TRUE
BELIEVER

ALEXANDER

BOLOTNIKOV

AS TOLD TO

GINA WAHLEN

REVIEW AND HERALD® PUBLISHING ASSOCIATION
HAGERSTOWN, MD 21740

The author assumes full responsibility for the accuracy of all facts and quotations as cited in this book. Because of the sensitive nature of some of the material in this book, some of the names and circumstances were changed or modified.

Passages credited to Avos are from *Pirkei Avos/Ethics of the Fathers*. © Copyright 1984 by Mesorah Publications, Ltd. All rights reserved.

Scripture quotations marked NASB are from the *New American Standard Bible*, © The Lockman Foundation 1960, 1962, 1963, 1968, 1971, 1972, 1973, 1975, 1977.

Texts credited to NIV are from the *Holy Bible, New International Version*. Copyright © 1973, 1978, 1984, International Bible Society. Used by permission of Zondervan Bible Publishers.

Texts credited to NKJV are from The New King James Version. Copyright © 1979, 1980, 1982 by Thomas Nelson, Inc. Used by permission. All rights reserved.

This book was
Edited by Gerald Wheeler
Copyedited by Jocelyn Fay and James Cavil
Cover design by Willie S. Duke
Interior design by Patricia S. Wegh
Typeset: 10/14 Aries

PRINTED IN U.S.A.

01 00 99 98 97   10 9 8 7 6 5 4 3 2 1

R&H Cataloging Service
Bolotnikov, Alexander
    True believer, by Alexander Bolotnikov as told to Gina Wahlen.

1. Bolotnikov, Alexander.   I. Wahlen, Gina.   II. Title.
        [B]   920.0092924

ISBN 0-8280-1301-2

DEDICATION

This book is dedicated to the memory of the 100,000 men, women, and children mercilessly slaughtered at Babi Yar in Kiev, Ukraine.

ACKNOWLEDGMENTS

I would like to thank Alexander ("Sasha") for sharing his story with me and giving me the privilege of helping him present it to the rest of the world. I also want to thank his wife, Irina, who proofread the manuscript, calling our attention to details, and who prepared all the photographs.

Special thanks also go to Pastor J. R. Spangler for his interest and strong support for this book. Thanks also to Tim Crosby and the Review and Herald® Publishing Association.

I also want to thank my husband, Clinton, who spent hours reading the manuscript and suggested editorial changes. And finally, I thank our 4-year-old son, Daniel, who played many hours with his baby-sitters, Julia and Vadim Dementyev, while Mommy worked on the book.

FOREWORD

Many times in life something will happen that seems unimportant at the moment. But it may be a decision that forever alters the course of one's life. Or it may be a chance meeting with some individual—an encounter that at first appears insignificant but later ends up with you standing at the altar declaring, "I do!" Even a wrong turn while driving on the highway may avert a tragedy that we will learn about only after our Lord returns. Some call these "insignificant" events fate, but true believers consider them to be providential.

My encounter with Alexander Bolotnikov was definitely providential. At the time I first met him, Sasha—to use his nickname—was just another person among the thousands I encountered during the evangelistic thrust our church conducted in the former U.S.S.R.

As I look back at our "chance" meeting in Kiev, Ukraine, in 1991, I am astounded at my unawareness of the importance of our initial introduction. Today I barely remember his approaching me at the end of my meeting in the beautiful cathedral called the House of Organ Music. To think that out of that large audience of several thousand, most of whom were standing, the Holy Spirit was leading one Jewish lad about 19 years of age to seek me out and ask which Christian church he should join.

Now I know for a certainty that from our Lord's viewpoint, that meeting was not only important, but had far-reaching consequences for our church. Little did I realize that our introduction would lead to Bolotnikov's further education at Andrews University, where he received his master's degree in biblical languages, a place on our Bible Translation Institute team, and a faculty position teaching Hebrew at our Zaokski Seminary in Russia.

Sasha and his wife, Irina, are indeed precious jewels. He has a sweet, unselfish spirit and a healthy sense of humor. Above all, he is a most teachable person and a willing learner. A fine speaker, he easily captivates his audience and is an excellent translator. His life of being first a devoted Communist, then a devout Jew, and finally a committed Seventh-day Adventist Christian is nothing less than miraculous.

I have often compared Sasha's life to that of the apostle Paul. Both Paul and Sasha were born of full-blooded Jewish parents. He did not know at first that Hasidic rabbinical blood ran in his veins. His roots trace to the nineteenth century in Palestine, where several of his ancestors were Hasidic rabbis. Sasha did not know his background until the Lord used Communism to strike him down—but not with a blazing flash of light. Rather a Communist decree forever changed the direction of his life. His story will convince all that we have a loving God who is intensely and personally interested in each one of us.

—J. R. Spangler, assistant to Mark Finley, speaker/
director, It Is Written television ministry.

CHAPTER 1

LENIN IS ALWAYS
ALIVE,
LENIN IS ALWAYS
WITH YOU,
IN HOPE, IN SORROW,
AND IN JOY.
LENIN IS IN
YOUR DREAMS,
IN EVERY HAPPY MOMENT.
LENIN IS IN
YOU
AND IN ME!

The words easily rolled off my tongue as I sang the Communist Young Pioneer theme song chorus. A true believer, I saw at last that my dreams were coming to pass. The Young Pioneer leaders were going to invest me with the highest honor a 10-year-old Soviet child could receive—the red scarf signifying that I was a member of the Communist Party's organization for children ages 10-13.

The investiture of new Pioneers was a grand occasion that took place in the sacred Lenin's Room, a place normally kept locked except for very special ceremonies. It was the first time I had been in such a place, and I could feel a sense of awe as I quietly stepped into the hushed room. Everything was red and gold—red curtains, red flags, red banners, all trimmed in gold. And pictures hung everywhere—photographs of Lenin as a child, Lenin as a youth, Lenin as a young adult, Lenin as a man. Lenin was everywhere. Display cases highlighted some of the great works of Lenin, and his 54-volume set of written works lined the wall. Truly Lenin was a great man, I decided, and I was proud to be following in his footsteps.

I was also following the footsteps of my parents and grandparents, all active Communist Party members. It was a choice my grandparents had made years earlier. Born in Russia before the 1917 revolution, they faced a difficult life, not only because they were poor, but because they were Jews. They knew all too well the Russian hostility against Jews and the terrible pogroms carried out by the czars that massacred tens of thousands of Jews across the country.

Looking for a way out of this terrible life of persecution, they believed that they had found it when a young man by the name of Vladimir Ilyich Lenin appeared on the scene. "Forsake your God and the faith of your fathers, and I will set you free," he promised.

My grandparents made their choice—they abandoned their Jewish background and became atheists and members of the Communist Party. My grandfather became a colonel in the KGB (the Soviet Union's secret police force).

However, my grandparents' decision to become atheists did not free me from anti-Semitic attitudes, as I was soon to learn. But for the time being I plunged wholeheartedly into my new life as a member of the Young Pioneers and took very seriously the solemn pledge I made "to love the motherland deeply, to live, study, and struggle according to the great Lenin's behests and the Communist Party's teachings, as well as to comply with the Rules of Soviet Pioneers." Some of the rules included:

"A Pioneer is loyal to the motherland, the Party, and Communism.

"A Pioneer honors the memory of fallen fighters and prepares to become a defender of the Motherland.

"A Pioneer is an honest and good friend, and comes out bravely in defense of truth.

"A Pioneer is a friend to Pioneers and children all over the world."[1]

Even before becoming a Pioneer, I enjoyed listening to the *Dawning of the Pioneers,* a radio program that came on each morning at 7:40. Every day I awoke to the sound of a trumpet blaring the Pioneer song, followed by the greeting "Hello, boys and girls. Listen to the Pioneer's *Dawn.*" Eagerly I would run to the breakfast table, where I would eat and enjoy hearing the Pioneer stories at the same time.

"Boys and girls, today we are going to talk about the word 'pioneer.' The word 'pioneer' means 'first'—the one who is on the front line, and who is followed by other people. These are the people who go to places where no one has ever lived. There they build a new city. These are pioneers. They came first and the others came after them.

"Think of the first people on the first spaceships, going into space. They are pioneers. So why do we call children 'pioneers'? They are not building cities and are not flying into space. Today these children are studying at school, but after several years the Soviet country will be built by their hands. They are the people of the future.

"When the great October Revolution [in 1917] took over, the children, of course, wanted to partake in the building of a new life. But they didn't know how to help adults. According to the advice of Lenin, and his wife, Nadezhda,[2] the young Communists organized the first children's units in Moscow. They called them the Pioneers. This work was going really well, and on May 19, 1922, the Communists decided to organize this work all around the country. Now there are hundreds of thousands of these units all around the world, named in honor of Lenin.

"Soviet Pioneers have their own symbols: a banner, a scarf, a badge, and a salute. We remember those who died for the revolution, and those who were on the war fronts defending our country. That's why the banners are red like blood. The red scarf is a reflection of the banner. Together with the scarf, Pioneers wear a badge. On this badge we have a portrait of Lenin with the words 'Always ready.'

"When children are accepted as Pioneers, they make a solemn pledge and give a salute. The salute is a greeting for the young followers of Lenin. The hand placed above the head is a sign that the interests of society are more important than personal interests. Five fingers held together is a sign of friendship with the children of the workers of the five continents. When the anthem of the Soviet Union is played, the Pioneer must give a salute. A salute is also to be given to the Pioneer banner and to memorials of the heroes of those who died during the revolution and the Great Patriotic War [World War II]."[3]

With such information filling my mind and heart, I would run off to school, where we would have more Pioneer activities. Each week we would have special Pioneer meetings. Appointed as my group's "political informer," I had the privilege each week of reporting the political events of the Soviet Union and the world. Eagerly I scanned the pages of our Soviet newspapers, *Pravda* and *Izvestia*, looking for the choicest news items. Week after week I would extol the peacekeeping virtues of Leonid Brezhnev and condemn the warmongers of the imperialistic West—particularly of the United States and its president, Ronald Reagan.

"All Americans are not bad," I declared. "The problem is their giant military complex. America has huge factories that manufacture weapons. These factories are run by capitalists, who are very rich. They want to make more and more money, so they keep producing lots of weapons. America won't cut their weapons production, because the capitalists refuse to shut down their factories! While these capitalists are very wealthy, the rest of the population is extremely poor. This is why we need to educate the workers in

America how to have a Communist revolution, and then the whole world will start moving toward the great and bright Communistic future."

In the evening I enjoyed taking out the large world map and counting how many countries were in the "Communist socialist fraternity." I counted Bulgaria, Romania, Poland, and other European countries. Then I would go to Africa and check Angola, Libya, Algeria, Syria, Iraq, and other hospitable places. I could hardly wait until the rest of the world joined hands with these intelligent countries.

One article in *Pravda* in 1982 really touched my heart. It told how the country of Paraguay had put the leader of its Communist Party, Antonio Maydana, in prison. The article reported eyewitness accounts of how Comrade Maydana had been shoved into a dark cell. The police had put a dark sack over his head so that he could not see. Then they had tortured him with electricity and fire. The newspaper told us that the torture was designed to make Comrade Maydana deny his Communist convictions and ideas. The article appealed for all Pioneers of the Soviet Union to go door-to-door on May 20 to obtain signatures from the people. These signatures would be gathered together in one great book and sent to the government of Paraguay with a demand to set the leader of its Communist Party free.

Moved by this shocking account, I eagerly went door-to-door and personally gathered 3,000 signatures. We never heard what happened to Comrade Maydana.

Another exciting event in the life of a Pioneer was the annual Lenin's Communist Sabbath that took place during the week of Lenin's birthday. During my first year as a Pioneer I eagerly anticipated this opportunity to help spread Communism throughout the world. The authorities told us that during this day we would work for a salary, and that all of our salary would go into the

Soviet Peace Fund. Money from this fund would help Libyan revolutionaries struggle against American imperialism.

Finally the day arrived. Our leaders told us to go from door to door, asking people to give us their recyclable paper. It was a great day. Some of the Pioneers collected 500 pounds of paper. All the paper we had enthusiastically gathered we put into a gazebo near the school. Every day we anxiously waited to see if the truck would come to pick up the paper and take it to the factory. But to our disappointment it just sat there for three months, until it went up in smoke from someone's burning cigarette butt.

While I experienced little disappointments here and there, I was still waiting for the fulfillment of my greatest desire—to attend one of the great Pioneer youth camps. I had my heart set on going to camp, and the stories I heard on my favorite radio program, *Dawning of the Pioneers,* fueled it even more.

"Let's go on a little journey to Camp Artek," one program began, "where you, along with 5,000 other Pioneers, will spend your summer vacation on the edge of the Black Sea. Let's get acquainted with the place where we will live for 26 days. In the evening, near the campfire, we will meet all the children in our unit. Everyone will tell about himself or herself, his or her hobbies, and what he or she wants to do during camp. On the grand opening day there will be a celebrity lineup. The flag will be raised, and the season will start. Now the great fun begins. We will listen to a concert in the Pioneer theater. We will participate in sports competitions, and after supper everyone will gather near the campfire and sing their favorite songs. The next morning we'll go hiking to the forest or to the river. In the afternoon we'll divide into small groups. Which group is really interesting to you? The circle of artists? of technicians? of cosmonauts?

"On the fifth day, during morning lineup, there is an announcement: 'Today will be a water holiday.' Our special guest will be Neptune. When everyone is at the beach, we suddenly hear the sound of a trumpet. It is heralding from the fleet of the great king of the sea. Accompanying him are several mermaids and water monsters. The holiday finishes late in the evening. On another day we have time to work on a special farm. The neighboring village is waiting for our help. And then in the evening we have a surprise—our camp counselors invite all Pioneers to a special concert. The next day we will go hiking for two days. The older Pioneers will carry the tents. After the hike there will be an exhibition of pictures taken on the trip.

"A few days later, during the morning lineup, the flag of the Olympic Games is raised. We will have a sports holiday. We will compete in jumping, running, and swimming, and those who win will get special prizes.

"On the final day of camp we will have a great carnival to end our wonderful time here. Goodbye, Artek. We will never forget you. You gave us many joyful days and many good friends."

I was ready to go and begged my mother to get me an entrance ticket to Artek. But she didn't know how. In fact, no one from my school or town seemed to know how to get tickets for Artek. They simply were not available—not to us, anyway. With approximately 30 million Pioneers across the Soviet Union begging to go to Artek, entrance tickets were prize possessions—reserved only for children living in the big cities such as Moscow and Kiev, and for children of Communist Party leaders.

But I didn't give up. I really wanted the joy of experiencing a Pioneer camp firsthand, and I had heard that other Pioneer camps existed. So I said, "Mom, I want to go to any camp, as long as it is really good and nice and looks like Artek."

So my mother began the great search. Tickets were easily available to camps other than Artek, and my mother checked out each one carefully. Was it similar to Artek? Did it offer the same activities? Were the facilities comparable? What about the general program? From her investigations my mother learned that a camp near Moscow would be the best place for me to get an "Artek experience." So she obtained the ticket, and I went for 26 days to spend a happy summer.

My mom and I took the overnight train to Moscow. The following morning we went to a special meeting point on the northwest side of Moscow, where excited kids from all around the Soviet Union gathered to begin their great camp adventure. We told our mothers goodbye and climbed onto the bus that would transport us 60 miles (100 kilometers) farther west, a site in the middle of a forest.

I was expecting something really adventurous. Peering out the window for my first view of the camp, I saw several two-story buildings in an area surrounded by a high fence with a large gate, and a big forest beyond. This was it.

We got out of the bus and divided into units according to age. I was in the 11-year-old category. Each unit had a counselor assigned to it. The counselors were 19- and 20-year-olds on their summer break from pedagogical institutes (teacher-training schools).

After being put into units, we marched to the long two-story building that would be our home for the next 26 days. Inside, the building had 10 rooms on each floor, with 10 beds per room. The community bathroom was located at the end of the long hallway.

Quickly choosing a bunk and putting my few things away, I sat down, waiting for the great fun to begin. Soon it was suppertime, and we went to the camp cafeteria. Sitting down to eat, I could hardly believe what I was looking at. There on my plate was a slab of fat (the cooks had stolen the meaty part). Beside the fat was kasha—a kind of wheat mush that had already hardened. In fact, it was so hard that with one swoop of my fork I could lift the entire portion off the plate. Next to the petrified kasha were tomatoes that looked as if they had been in "hot storage" since the previous year. Hard, several-day-old bread complemented the spread. After the meal I went to bed, hoping for a great tomorrow.

---

[1] N. V. Kraselnekova, T. E. Melenteva, E. E. Morozova, and G. B. Potapova, *Learning to Read Russian: A Teach-Yourself Book for Schoolchildren* (Moscow: Russky Yazyk Publishers, 1988), p. 295.

[2] In Russian *Nadezhda* (or *Nadia)* means "hope."

[3] Kraselnekova, pp. 295-298.

CHAPTER 2

At 7:00 a.m. sharp the bugle blared the familiar Pioneer anthem, followed by a voice shouting over the intercom, "Get up, young Pioneers! Get up! Get up, young Pioneers! Get up!" The voice continued to shout as I leaped out of bed. The thought went through my mind that this experience was similar to a movie I had seen about Auschwitz, where the Nazis had imprisoned the Jews. Quickly brushing the similarity aside, I hurried to get cleaned up and dressed.

Rushing into the hallway, we lined up by units. "And now we are going to march," the senior counselor announced. "Attention! Right face. Ready, march!" Then we went out the door and around a big circle for two hours. Hungry, I thought the ordeal would never end. I wondered if the Pioneers at Artek had to march so much.

Finally we stopped. "Today each unit will select a commander," the senior counselor said. "Every morning the commanders will take attendance and report to me when your unit is lined up and ready for the day." Afterward the anthem of the Soviet Union played, we gave our salutes, and someone raised the red flag. At last they dismissed us for a terrible breakfast.

After breakfast things were strangely quiet. Where were our counselors? What about the great activities that we had heard so much about? What about games, hiking, concerts, swimming, and all the other fun things we were supposed to be enjoying? Since the counselors had apparently evaporated, we went looking for something to do. Discovering a soccer field and basketball court, we decided to play. But where were the balls? At last we found someone we could ask, and were told that "all balls are given out only by the special command of the camp chief." He assured us that we would eventually get to use them, but did not know exactly when.

Since it was impossible to play soccer or basketball without a ball, we turned our attention to the surrounding forest and the river located just a couple hundred yards from the front gate. We decided that maybe this would be a good place to go. But as we approached the gate, our hopes dropped into the pit of our stomachs as a big bully of a man stepped out of the guardhouse and began swearing at us. "If any of you _____ kids steps on the other side of this _____ gate, you will soon find out how much one of these _____ fists weighs." He shook his fist in our faces. So we turned around with the sickening realization that we were trapped. There was nothing we could do.

Soon it was lunchtime. Our counselors reappeared, and we sat down to a lunch of watery borscht and stale bread. A thick layer of lard floated on top of the borscht, replacing the meat chunks supposed to be there. A couple lonely pieces of potato swam around in the lard. The food was definitely not improving.

After lunch our counselors again disappeared, leaving us once more on our own. We decided to go exploring around the buildings, and discovered some locked game rooms. Peering through the dusty windows, we could see a room that appeared to be in a perpetual state of disrepair, with no table games, no card games, no library, and not much of anything but a mess.

By this time we were really bored. At least the girls had some chalk, and so they had drawn squares on the pavement and began playing hopscotch. But what could we boys do? We sat down and talked.

The disappearance of the counselors mystified me and the other younger campers. The older boys grinned and started to explain where the counselors were, using words that I had never heard before. They laughed when I asked their meaning. After a while they led me, along with the other 11-year-olds, to the locked counselor rooms. Peering through the keyhole, I discovered how Young Pioneers got their sex education. For the next few minutes 10 boys persistently pushed and shoved, trying to get a peek through the keyhole. This turned out to be the most exciting thing at Pioneer Camp.

Occasionally in the evening a special guest would come from the KGB and tell us political information. But what they said was always predictable—Brezhnev was trying to save the world while Reagan was trying to destroy it.

The days and nights slowly eked by in a never-ending cycle of early-morning marching, horrible meals, and intense boredom. After the eighth morning of marching for two hours, followed by another revolting breakfast, I decided that enough was enough. Ready to go home, I took out a pen and some graph paper and wrote:

"Dear Mama,

"This place is terrible. The food is awful, and there is nothing to do. I'm hungry and bored. All the kids hate this place. Please come get me right away. I want to go home.

"Sasha"

After several days I received a reply:

"Dear Sasha,

"Just wait a little while longer. You have only two more weeks, and the days will go by quickly.

"Mama"

It was not the answer I wanted to hear. A lump rose in my throat as tears silently rolled down my face. I wanted to go home.

Then it happened. On day 17 of my incarceration at Pioneer Camp the most beautiful person in the world appeared—my mother! As I quickly packed my bag I could hear the comments of other campers: "Wish I was getting out of here too!" "Hey, pack me in that suitcase." "Maybe they'll let me out with your mother!"

As I left camp that day, I realized that the dawning of my Pioneer experience had already turned into a sunset. My next great hope was to become a member of Komsomol—the Communist Party's youth organization. Surely all of Communism's promises would come true then.

CHAPTER 3

Who will be turning 14 years old by the end of December?" my homeroom teacher asked one day. Along with several others in my class, I raised my hand. It was a lie, but I decided that I had waited long enough to join the Komsomol organization. Besides, my birthday was in March, just three months past the deadline for this group.

"You may now begin the process of becoming Komsomol members," the teacher informed us. "It is a high honor to become a Komsomolite, and you must prepare carefully," she continued. We were to read the complete 54-volume set of Lenin's writings, making careful and detailed notes, as well as study some of the works of Karl Marx and other great lights of Communism. At the end of the three-month preparation process we were to present our knowledge and pass a rigorous exam.

Eagerly I dove into the literature of Communism. Reading Marx, Engels, and Lenin, the warmth in my heart grew into a fire as I understood more and more clearly what the world would be like once all the workers of the world united.

After three months of vigorous preparation and intense study, I was ready for the exam. Then, just a day before the long-awaited examination, the leaders asked us to present our birth certificates. My heart sank as I hoped the examiners wouldn't notice my birth date: March 23, 1971. But they did notice. It was another three long months before I could apply again to become a Komsomolite, and another bitter disappointment in my quest to become a full-fledged Communist.

At last my fourteenth birthday arrived, and I received my red-and-gold Komsomol membership card. Now that I was finally in, I immediately began looking for ways to further the goals of Communism.

Since I had served as the "political informer" for my Pioneer group, it was natural that I should continue the role in the Komsomol. Each day I carefully read the pages of *Komsomolskaya Pravda* and *Izvestia,* searching for the latest information to present to my Komsomol group.

I felt good about the contributions I was making and was happy to be forwarding the goals of Communism. Then one day a bomb hit me. Not a real bomb, of course, but something just about as devastating to my understanding of Communism. The discovery came packaged in my grandfather's suitcase.

My *dedushka*[1] had spent the last two years of his life lying on a bed in our apartment, where he died in May 1984. He never left his bed unless it was absolutely necessary. It wasn't that he couldn't physically get up—a deep case of depression had chained him down.

After renouncing Judaism and embracing Communism at the time of the revolution, Dedushka became a rising star in the Communist Party and quickly rose to the top, where he held the rank of colonel in the KGB for decades. A good Communist, he did his work well. Consequently, he trusted no one, and no one trusted him. Then at the age of 52 he received orders to retire. Joseph Stalin was busy sweeping out all Jews from government positions, no matter what rank they held or how many decades they had served. Suddenly Dedushka found himself without an identity and without friends. He experienced profound grief over his betrayal by a system to which he had dedicated his life.

A few weeks after his death I noticed two of his suitcases tucked away in a corner of our apartment. "What do you think is inside Dedushka's suitcases?" I asked my mother.

"I don't know. Let's find out," she replied, also curious to learn what her father had saved from his 84 years of existence.

We brought out a suitcase and set it on the bed. Opening the suitcase was like unlocking the past. Laid out before us were various medals Dedushka had been awarded, his Communist Party and KGB identification cards, and his service record, showing his abrupt retirement in 1952. As my mother and I carefully walked through the past, my eye suddenly caught something familiar—the bold masthead of *Pravda,* the official newspaper of the Communist Party. *What's this doing in here?* I wondered as I picked up the yellowed paper. Immediately I could tell that it was a special edition—one seen only by high-ranking Communist officials. I knew that it had never been distributed to the general Soviet population, because it had no date printed on it. The Communist Party had decided this issue contained information they didn't want the people to read.

On the front page was a letter from Premier and General Secretary Nikita Khrushchev. It discussed sending missiles and troops to Cuba. Reading the letter, I became more and more agitated. "Comrades," Khrushchev said in it, "there is an important work to be done. With these missiles in Cuba we are now able to bring down American imperialism forever." It shocked me. I had never heard of this kind of aggression by the Soviet Union. *What about the Soviet Peace Fund that worked to keep out American aggression?* I wondered.

The letter went completely against what I had learned in my history classes. We had been taught that Soviet arms and technicians had gone to Cuba to defend the country from an imminent American invasion. It was purely a defensive action, they had assured us.

Which was true? They couldn't both be right. It would take me more than a year to decide, but one night at the dinner table the answer arrived.

My parents' best friends, Mikhail and Galena, had come over, and we were sitting around the table discussing recent discoveries made possible through Gorbachev's *glasnost.*[2] The whole country was in a state of shock as we learned about Stalin's atrocities—20 million Soviets starved to death during the great five-year plans of farm collectivization, 20 million more starving and being worked to death in labor camps.

Then somehow the Cuban missile crisis came up. *"Da,"* Mikhail said. "A close friend of mine was in the Soviet Army at that time. In fact, he was in one of the units sent to Cuba as a 'specialist.' The special units in Cuba received a letter from Khrushchev telling them that the important work they were doing with the missiles would bring down American imperialism forever."

The letter! Suddenly I realized that Mikhail was quoting from the very letter I had read in Dedushka's undistributed issue of *Pravda.* So it was true. Khrushchev had planned to attack the United States. It went against everything I had ever read from Lenin's teachings. I decided that I must present the truth to my Komsomol group.

On April 21, 1985—Lenin's birthday—I presented my searing

discovery to my Komsomol group. I had chosen the date deliberately. What better day to bring forward the true meaning of
Lenin's teachings than on his birthday?

I entitled my presentation "How Our Soviet Leaders Have Not
Followed Lenin's Teachings." "Comrades," I began, "today I am
going to share with you an important discovery I have made. A discovery that shows how Premier Nikita Khrushchev did not follow
the teachings of Lenin. In 1962 he placed Soviet nuclear missiles in
Cuba to threaten the U.S.A. My friends, Lenin did not teach us to
act like this. We know that American imperialism is very aggres-
sive, but we cannot behave like them. All progressive countries in
the world are looking at us. We have to be an example of peace-
keepers, the people of goodwill for all the world. This is the command of Lenin. Khrushchev did not follow this command, and
now we are reaping a bitter harvest. Americans have put their missiles in Western Europe. I believe that this happened because we
gave them a bad example."

The room was silent. Vladimir Fyodorovich, our homeroom
teacher, sat in the back of the room, his face as white as the snow
in January. The meeting dismissed. "Better be careful," some whis-
pered to me as they left. Nothing more was said.

A few days later Fyodorovich[3] wanted to see me. In addition to
being the homeroom teacher, he was also my physics teacher. I
liked him, and we had a good relationship. He let the students call
him "Vef."

"Look," Vef said, "you have a good possibility of having a great
scientific career in front of you. You are an excellent student, and
you enjoy physics and do well in it. I have great hopes for you.

"But I also know you enjoy politics. Politics and science don't
mix. They both take a lot of time, and to be good, you must be totally dedicated to either one or the other.

"Sasha," he continued, "you're going to have to choose—either science or politics. If you choose science, I will do everything I can to help you succeed. I'll help you learn everything there is to know about physics. And I'll help you get accepted to one of the best scientific institutes in the country. But if you choose politics, there's nothing I can do. You'll be on your own."

I made my choice, resigning as the "political informer" of my Komsomol group but remaining a loyal member. I would be a physicist like Vef. Admiring him, I wanted to be like him. My special interest was in nuclear physics, and Vef encouraged me. I read the theories of Einstein, Bohr, and other great scientists. I wanted to make great scientific discoveries and create huge spaceships that would fly faster than the speed of light. Having a burning desire to understand the secrets of matter, I believed that somehow through the secrets of science we would be able to accomplish Lenin's vision of worldwide peace.

---

[1] *Dedushka* is the Russian word for grandfather. The more familiar word *babushka* refers to grandmother.

[2] In Russian *glasnost* means "openness."

[3] In Russian it is a sign of respect to call a person by their first name and patronymic, rather than with the title "Mr.," "Mrs.," or "Miss," followed by their last name. The patronymic derives from the person's father's name (in this case, "Feyodor"), followed by "ovich" for men and "ovna" for women.

CHAPTER 4

She walked into the classroom, and immediately the room hushed. Our new history teacher, Svetlana Andreyevna, had arrived. The woman seemed to tower over us with her five-foot-seven-inch wide-body frame, her blue eyes whisking quickly up and down the rows of our tenth-grade class. The wife of a high-ranking KGB officer, Svetlana Andreyevna was someone not to tangle with.

Picking up the attendance list, she began to read. "Svetlana Polyanskaya?"

"*Ya!*" came the answer.

"Yuri Balalin?"

"*Ya!*"

Soon she came to my name. "Alexander Bolotnikov?"

"*Ya!*" I responded.

She paused, then said, "Alexander Bolotnikov, do you know that you have the same last name as Ivan Bolotnikov, the Russian who rebelled against the czar in the 1600s in order to free the peasants?"

Proudly I announced that my

grandfather had changed his last name to Bolotnikov in honor of this great man, who was a Communist before his time. This bit of information intrigued Svetlana Andreyevna, and she wrote down something on the class record. Since it was common knowledge that many Jews had changed their last names after the revolution, I realized that she probably knew I was Jewish. The roll call continued, and she said nothing more about it that day.

"Our textbook for the class is *History of the U.S.S.R.*," Svetlana announced. "It is an excellent and comprehensive work, and I hope you will become thoroughly acquainted with it. In it you will study further the works of Lenin and others who helped lead the glorious revolution. You will carefully read each assignment from the book and be prepared to give a full report on your reading, as well as answer any questions about it." After she gave us a reading assignment, she dismissed the class.

The next day her eyes coolly roamed the classroom until they came to rest on my face. "Bolotnikov!" she snapped. "Come to the front of the class. Let's see how smart you are."

Without hesitating I went up front. Loving history almost as much as physics, I had read the assignment and was well prepared. "So, what have you got to tell us?" she challenged. Eagerly I began a long recitation of what I had learned from the assigned reading. "OK! OK!" Svetlana interrupted. "So you think you're so smart, do you? Well, what about this?" she demanded, asking a question not related to the reading assignment. Drawing on my previous historical knowledge, I answered correctly. Another question, then another and another. After apparently answering them satisfactorily, I was sent back to my seat. Her brusque, sarcastic attitude puzzled me.

The next day she repeated the process. "Bolotnikov," she said, "you were prepared very nicely yesterday. Let's see how systematic you are in your preparation. Come to the front of the class!"

Again I stood. Again I answered her questions, but she frowned at each correct response I gave. Her disappointment puzzled me, but I said nothing. After a couple more times of these strange encounters, she did not call me up again for the rest of the quarter.

In addition to the class periods in which the students would regurgitate what they had learned from the history book, we also had lectures and class discussions. I remember one of the first such lessons. The topic was "proper Communist dress and adornment." Our teacher told us we should follow certain definite rules.

"The true Communist will demonstrate his or her beliefs by what he or she wears," Svetlana Andreyevna declared. "This will show what kind of morals he or she really has. The true Communist will wear only the good-quality, attractive clothing that our Soviet factories manufacture. What other country produces such nice, long, warm winter coats, durable trousers for men, and sensible dresses for women? What other country has such nice school pinafores for the girls to wear and practical clothes for boys? You can tell a true Communist by the clothes he or she wears!" she announced. We silently stared at her soft, stylishly cut dress and matching leather shoes. It was like no Soviet outfit we had ever seen.

"On the other hand," she continued, "what kind of people would even think of wearing the provocative, immoral clothes produced by the hands of the exploited workers in the West? What kind of people will pay a year's salary to buy expensive sports shoes or—worst of all—blue jeans on the black market?"

The class remained silent. "I'll tell you what kind of people!" she exploded. "People with no morals. People who don't care if they're exploiting poor workers who had to piece together these garments for the rich!

"And tell me," she demanded, "where would people get $250 for a pair of jeans? Where are they getting that kind of money?

Our government graciously pays you a decent salary, but who is paying you that kind of money? What secret alliance do you have?" she asked. "You see, when people wear Western clothing, or jewelry, or makeup, it forces us to ask these kinds of questions." I noticed her ruby-red lips, silently wondering where she got her lipstick.

"These corrupted styles are the mark of the West! We don't have to look like the West. There is absolutely no good in the West. They are our enemies!

"But can you imagine," she continued, her tone now more smooth and subtle, with a touch of sarcasm, "there are actually people in the Soviet Union who try to emigrate to the West?" The class was silent. "These people are very bad, with no morals."

Then, turning to where I was sitting, Svetlana Andreyevna addressed me. "Sasha, do you know that there are many Jews who emigrate to Israel?" A slight smile curled the corners of her lips. Everyone stared at me.

"Yes," I replied. "I have heard about this. But what relationship does it have to me and my family? My parents are both loyal and active Communists. My father is the vice-director of the company that builds nuclear power plants. My grandparents supported Lenin during the revolution. And my grandfather was a KGB officer. I have no desire or plans to emigrate, nor does my family. So what does this question have to do with me?" I waited for her reply.

Ignoring my question completely, she continued right where she had left off. "These are very bad people. They emigrate to Israel, but then they realize how bad off they are. They plead for our Soviet government to allow them to come back, and graciously our government agrees. But then the government has to take care of them—give them apartments, a good job, free medical care, free schools—all of the benefits they trampled on when they left the Soviet Union."

She continued her pontification. "These are great privileges our government gives us, but these Jews don't consider such things a privilege. Nevertheless, when they want to come back, the government has to accept them again. This is very offensive to the government."

Totally shocked, I sat quietly at my desk, not knowing what to say or do. The teacher's sarcastic smile spread to the lips of many of my classmates. It was my first direct experience with anti-Semitism, and it left me sick to my stomach. Mercifully, the class period ended. I was glad Vef's physics class was next. At least he accepted me for what I was.

Several weeks passed with no further antagonistic remarks. Then came the day when we would again visit the sacred Lenin Room and have a complete tour with Svetlana Andreyevna. I had not been in this special room since my investiture as a Pioneer five years earlier.

It looked exactly as I had remembered it, with everything decorated in red and gold. Pictures of Lenin still covered the walls, and his books still filled the bookcases. Display cases featured various manuscripts and artifacts. A sense of awesomeness still pervaded the room's atmosphere.

"You will notice," Svetlana Andreyevna announced, "that the articles in this room are arranged in three groups—Lenin as a child, as a young revolutionary, and as the leader of the Soviet Union."

Leading us to the section featuring Lenin's childhood, she pointed out a picture of an angelic-looking little Lenin. "Even as a child, Vladimir Ilyich showed extraordinary potential. Such an honest child."

We moved on to the revolutionary Lenin. "It was as a student at the University of Kazan, on the Volga River, that Vladimir Ilyich first read the writings of Karl Marx and was excited to catch a glimmer of hope." Then our teacher quoted from Marx's *Communist*

Manifesto: "Communists everywhere support every revolutionary movement against the existing social and political order of things. . . . They openly declare that their ends can be attained only by the forcible overthrow of all existing social conditions. Let the ruling classes tremble at a Communist revolution. The proletarians have nothing to lose but their chains. They have a world to win. Workingmen of all countries, unite!*

"Lenin had a great desire to help all the proletarians around the world lose their chains," Svetlana Andreyevna said, "but his time had not quite come."

She then directed our attention to a heart-wrenching painting showing Lenin trying to comfort his grief-stricken mother, who had just received the news that the czar had sentenced her eldest son to execution. His crime? Attempting to throw a bomb into the czar's carriage. He had hoped that killing the czar would overthrow the regime.

In the picture Lenin was trying to comfort his mother by telling her, "We will go another way."

"What he meant by this," our teacher said, "was that instead of just organizing terrorist acts, he would find a way to organize the crowds of workers and peasants into a powerful revolutionary group.

"Soon after this," Svetlana Andreyevna continued, "Lenin organized small study groups of workers. Every other evening these small groups would meet together and study the writings of Karl Marx, and each evening their hope would burn a little brighter. In fact, it was the power of these small groups that eventually led to the revolution! And, as you know, the czar sent him into exile for organizing these small study groups."

We walked over to a large display area featuring several photographs and documents. "Here you see several pictures of Lenin taken while he was in exile in Siberia in the 1890s. Lenin lived in a place called Shushenskoye," she explained.

One photograph looked especially intriguing, and I was glad when Svetlana Andreyevna pointed it out. "Look, students. Vladimir Ilyich continued his small group meetings even while in Siberia! Here we see a picture of Lenin and some Marxist friends who were also exiled because of their beliefs. Many of these men became great leaders in the revolution and in the new government of the Soviet Union."

Then suddenly her tone of voice changed. "However, one of these men was a traitor," she said, pointing to one of the faces in the photograph. Then she looked straight at me, and I wondered why. I didn't need to wonder for long. "This man's name was Martov," she continued, "and he was a Jew!" Every word she spoke was slow and deliberate. "He was the worst enemy of Lenin and tried to stop him from leading the revolution."

The entire class stared at me. Of course everyone knew that I was Jewish. It was as if she were driving a stake through my true-believing heart. I stood there, hot but silent.

Yet I also knew that Karl Marx himself was Jewish. Yakov Sverdlov, one of Lenin's best friends who served as the first Soviet minister of finance and industry, was Jewish. And Lev Trotsky, Lenin's defense minister, also was a Jew. In fact, I knew that 70 percent of Lenin's Communist government leaders were Jews, as well as my own grandparents, who had forsaken their entire Jewish heritage and history to become Communists.

In the very room where I had pledged "to love the motherland deeply, to live, study, and struggle according to the great Lenin's behests and the Communist Party's teachings," in the very place where I had promised bravely to defend truth, it was there that I felt the stinging bite of hypocrisy—and my faith began to waver.

---

* Karl Marx (1818-1883).

CHAPTER 5

I want to go home! I hate it here!" sobbed a distraught woman on the television screen. My family, along with most other families across the Soviet Union, were watching the Soviet-produced documentary *Former Citizens*. The government had widely advertised the film, and everyone I knew had planned to watch it. In the film Soviet journalists interviewed former Soviet citizens who had emigrated to the United States. The setting was New York City.

"I was deceived!" declared a clearly upset man in the film. "I was told that life would be wonderful here—that there would be more food than I could possibly eat, that I would live in a spacious home, that my family would be well cared for. Lies, lies, lies! Just take a look at where we live!" The camera slowly panned one of the ghettos of New York City. Garbage littered the alley. Graffiti covered the walls. Suspicious-looking people huddled in the corners.

"I don't feel safe here," the woman said. "How can I possibly allow my children to go out to play? Where can they play? We never realized how good the Soviet Union was to us, providing us with everything we needed—a good home, good schools, free medical care."

"Please tell people the truth," the man told the interviewing journalist. "Please tell them that anything good they have heard about the United States is a lie. The best country in the world is the U.S.S.R.!"

The next day in history class Svetlana Andreyevna pumped us for our reaction to the program. "What did you think about the movie you watched last night?" she asked.

All together we answered, "We don't want to emigrate to the United States. We love our country, and we are proud to be citizens of it."

Apparently the canned answer wasn't good enough for her. Pushing the probe a little deeper, she asked, "Will you *really* never want to go to the United States?"

We answered, "Never." But nothing we said seemed to satisfy her.

Again and again she kept repeating the question "Are you *sure* you never want to?"

At last she began to wear the class down, and finally someone answered, "Well, maybe it wouldn't be so bad just to go to the United States on a short visit, just as a tourist, but I'd *never ever* want to emigrate! It would just be interesting to see some of the rest of the world." The comment sparked a chain reaction, and soon many other students began expressing similar sentiments. It didn't take long for it to become a free-for-all discussion as more and more students echoed the idea. I remained silent, however, knowing that I needed to be especially careful about what I said and did around the woman.

Soon tears appeared in Svetlana Andreyevna's cool blue eyes.

Slowly they dropped, one by one, onto her smartly tailored jacket. "I'm really disappointed in you," she said, voice shaking. "I thought you were faithful citizens of our country! But now I see that all of my work, all of it, has gone down the drain." The tears continued to drop as she left the classroom for the principal's office. Once again I was glad Vef's physics class was next. I could do with a change of pace.

Vef strode into the classroom, his face ablaze with anger. He stood in front, staring at us. It shocked us. Never had we seen him so upset. "I have received information that you, as an entire class, behaved very badly during the last class period. You completely broke the discipline in the classroom, and you made your teacher cry." We were silent. Then Vef announced, "I do not want to begin our physics class while *Mr.* Bolotnikov[1] is present. There is nothing that I want to share with potential emigrants. Bolotnikov, leave the classroom immediately. You may not return to this class until I talk to your parents."

I picked up my books and left, realizing what had happened. Knowing that my teacher, whom I loved, had been deceived, I determined to provide him an explanation.

Waiting in the hallway during the 45-minute class period, I then went to Vef's office after the bell rang. "Vladimir Fyodorovich, may I talk with you for a minute?"

Looking up slowly, he asked, "What more can I say?"

"You don't have to say anything," I replied, "but I must tell you that this problem reveals Svetlana Andreyevna's anti-Semitic attitude, which is against the national policy of our Communist Party."

My words hit him between the eyes like a two-by-four. "What?" he asked. Suddenly the dam inside me broke and out poured all of the hurt, resentment, and confusion I had felt during the past several months of sitting in Svetlana Andreyevna's history class. I told Vef everything.

"I don't understand," I said. "She is supposed to be a representative of the Communist Party, but Lenin specifically taught *against* prejudice against the Jews. He's the one who stopped the czar's terrible pogroms. How can Svetlana Andreyevna be a model Communist and an anti-Semite?"

Shocked, Vef took me by the hand, and together we walked to where my class was having its next lesson. Apologizing to the teacher for having to interrupt, Vef went to the front. "I must make amends for my behavior during the last class period." The room was as silent as Lenin's tomb. "And I want to apologize publicly to Sasha Bolotnikov. I was misinformed about him and his behavior."

The class was amazed. Never had we seen anything like this. Vef continued, "Are there any students here who have witnessed Svetlana Andreyevna's words or behavior against Sasha personally or against Jews in general during the time in which you have known her?" Several students stood up. "You will go to the principal's office with me now, and you will testify about what you have observed," he declared. I could hardly believe my ears.

The next morning as I walked into the school building, Svetlana Andreyevna met me at the door. "I want to talk to you, Sasha," she said. "Please come with me." As soon as we walked into her office, she began to cry. "I'm sorry," she sobbed. "You probably misunderstood me." More sobs. "I have so many Jewish friends. I can't be an anti-Semite. You must have just misunderstood my words."

I repeated all the occasions when she had represented Jews in a negative light, and reminded her that many Jews were heroes of the Soviet Union—many were great revolutionaries, making up a large percentage of the government that Lenin formed.

She kept repeating her apologies about *my* "misunderstandings" and reminding me about her Jewish friends again and again for about two hours. Finally I said, "OK, I will forget about the problems between us and will not talk to anyone else about it."

Obviously relieved, she said, "Make sure that the principal knows that we have solved our problems."

Svetlana made no more anti-Semitic statements during history class. However, almost daily she would ask me in front of the class, "My dear little Sasha, have you been offended by anything that I've said in class today?"

Then in February 1985 I did something really stupid. It happened right after Svetlana Andreyevna's history class. A friend, also named Sasha, and I were laughing hysterically about what had taken place in history class that day.

The topic was Joseph Stalin and his great strategic abilities in the Great Patriotic War.[2] My friend Sasha had asked Svetlana Andreyevna if she knew what Stalin's real last name was. She answered, "Yes—it was Zhopareedza." The class absolutely exploded in laughter, not only because we knew Stalin's real name was Dzhugashoili, but because of a deeper reason Svetlana Andreyevna could not understand.

Because of our dislike for her, we had given her an uncomplimentary nickname that referred to her oversized posterior. What made it so extremely funny was the fact that her nickname, "Zhopareeda," and the name she had given for Stalin had exactly the same root word.

As my friend and I were walking down the hallway after class, talking and laughing, my eye caught a bright new poster on the bulletin board announcing an upcoming "Week of Support for Our Soldiers in Afghanistan." It declared in big, bold letters the person responsible for the activities for this special week of support: "SVETLANA ANDREYEVNA NICKOLAYEVA."

Sasha and I went into new spasms of laughter. Then I reached into my pocket and felt a black marking pen. The temptation was too great. Quickly grabbing the pen, I scribbled out her last name, Nickolayeva, and in its place hastily wrote "Zhopareedza." We could hardly stand up straight as we walked out the door laughing so hard.

The next day, however, all laughing stopped. Svetlana Andreyevna called my friend into her office. "I saw you yesterday and I know what happened," she told him. "I could really get you into bad trouble. But I don't want to have to do that. Listen. I know that you were not alone. If you tell me who else was with you, you'll go free, and that will be the end of it." So Sasha told her.

That afternoon she summoned me into the same office. "Listen, your friend told me everything that happened yesterday, and I know that this is your handwriting." She pulled out the poster. "You really made a mistake," she continued, "because I am the representative of the KGB in this school, and I already know what we're going to do. One day nicely dressed people will come into the school and copy your handwriting. Then they will write this word, using your handwriting, onto the bust of Lenin located in the school hallway. They will put the word you wrote on Lenin's forehead. Then you will be done away with. Forget about the universities you want to go to. Forget about your future." It was not a game, and I knew it. I also knew that she was dead serious and had the power to rip me out of school and away from my parents, put me in the army, and have me sent to Lake Baikal in Siberia, where temperatures drop to −50° F and the barracks are unheated. In addition to the frigid conditions, soldiers work alongside former criminals—a rough and vicious group. I knew a lot about it because a friend of mine, Vitaly, had been sent there and while on leave had told me all about it. After returning to Siberia, he had committed suicide.

As I stared down at the floor in Svetlana Andreyevna's office, thoughts of Vitaly grew in my mind. Never had I experienced such gripping fear. This woman had the power to ruin my life totally, and planned to use all of her influence to carry out her threat. Without saying a word, I walked out of her office.

Vef was distraught. "How could you do such a stupid thing, Sasha?" What could I say? By writing on that poster, I had defaced government property.

The next day Vef and I, along with three other outstanding physics students, went to Rovno, our regional center, to compete in a Physics Olympiad. The Olympiad was supposed to be an enjoyable and challenging time as the top physics students from throughout the region competed for the great honor of winning the Olympiad. The contest lasted for two of the longest weeks of my life. Fear consumed me as I continually wondered what was happening at my high school in Kuznetsovsk.

At last the Olympiad ended and we headed home. Returning to school the following day, I was greatly relieved to find Lenin's forehead just as clean as the day I had left. However, other things had been happening, and my friends quickly filled me in. A *militsinar* had repeatedly appeared at school and interrogated several of my classmates. While he apparently could not find whatever it was that he was looking for, he told several students, "We'll finally get this representative of Zionism." The KGB had opened a case against me. I was terrified.

Then one day my Ukrainian language teacher, who was also the vice principal, confidentially told me that I had another advocate—Tamara Petrovna, the school principal! Tamara Petrovna had gone personally to the local KGB director and had pleaded for them to drop my case.

I never knew for sure the final effects of my principal's pleading. Just eight weeks after I had scribbled my poster graffiti, a far more earthshaking event rocked the country. The Communist Party elected a new general secretary: Mikhail Sergeyevich Gorbachev.

A few weeks after the election, in May 1985, 40 million Soviet citizens, including myself, were glued to their television sets, listening to this radical new leader speak. "The reason we have so many economic problems in our country is that since the beginning of the 1970s the country has been in a state of stagnation," he said.

His statement was shocking in itself—it was the first time we had ever heard a Communist leader say that something was really wrong with our country. But Gorbachev went on: "We must accelerate the economic development of our country, and in order to do this we must create *perestroika* [restructuring]. We must do perestroika of our entire economic system, and this means we must have *glasnost* [openness]."

It was the first time I had heard such words as perestroika and glasnost. Of course, in a short time one would hear the two words around the world, but we did not yet realize what gigantic changes were packed into them.

Gorbachev's shocking speech continued. "We must develop the ability to look critically at our past as well as the present and find the truth." I knew what kind of truth he was talking about: the truth that the ideals set up by Lenin—that all men and women were equal and should have equal privileges—had been turned into a lie.

I had experienced this lie firsthand one day when my parents and I visited an old friend and classmate of my father's, an assistant to the prime minister of the Ukraine. He took us to his luxurious apartment, where just he and his wife lived. That in itself was quite a luxury, as it was typical in Soviet apartments to have two or three generations all crowding together in a small one- or two-bedroom apartment.

Our feet sunk into the thick, soft carpeting covering the floor.

The wallpaper was attractive and cheerful. The furniture was made of solid wood and thickly upholstered. When we saw how richly the man's apartment was furnished, we immediately wondered where and how he had been able to purchase such items. We had never seen anything of such high quality in the government-run state stores.

Turning to his friend, my father asked, "How much do you earn working for the prime minister?" Soviet culture did not consider such questions rude.

"Two hundred twenty rubles a month," the man answered. His reply shocked my father, because his salary was 340 rubles a month, but he could never decorate an apartment so elaborately.

Then the secret came out. Neither the prime minister nor his assistants shopped in the regular stores, my father's friend explained. There was a special store to which one had to have a special pass just to walk through the door. Once inside, it was like another world. Rows and rows of quality imported furniture lined the aisles. Everything one needed for the home was there. Lights, fixtures, wall coverings, carpeting, decorations, as well as chairs, couches, tables, beds, and other furniture. In addition to home furnishings, the store also had a complete line of Western clothing. But the most unbelievable part was the prices. A bedroom set that would cost $4,000 in the West would be just 350 rubles[3] at this special store. Men's designer suits, in the West normally $400, were just 80 rubles. Stereo systems worth $700 were on sale for only 150 rubles. It was a buyer's paradise and one absolutely off-limits to most Soviet citizens.

The experience engraved itself in my mind and added to my growing disaffection with the current state of Communism.

But Gorbachev seemed to be the savior I was looking for. He was the first to admit that many of our Soviet leaders had apostatized from the principles outlined in Lenin's plan for a perfect

Communist society—the society in which all nationalities would live together in peace, where all the riches of the world would be divided equally, and everyone would be fully satisfied.

To me, Lenin was the purest person in the world. I believed that he wanted a society in which honesty and fairness would reign. So when Gorbachev said, "We have to return to the original plans Lenin developed for our country," new hope rose in my heart. Here was the reformation I had been waiting for.

Nothing could stop me now. That summer Svetlana Andreyevna's husband received a promotion in the KGB, and they moved to another city. My final year of high school I spent studying hard and working with Vef as I prepared to enter the most prestigious scientific institute in the entire Soviet Union—the Moscow Institute of Physical Engineering, or simply MIPHE (pronounced MEE-fee) for short. There I would learn the secrets of nuclear physics. I would be able to understand and manipulate matter and help create a new, peaceful world.

My mother was not so optimistic. She told me about several cases in which well-qualified students had been denied entrance to prestigious universities simply because they were of Jewish descent. Then she shared with me her own personal experience with anti-Semitism. In 1960 she had graduated at the top of her class from the Kharkov Polytechnical University. One of the most prestigious military institutions in the country had invited her to apply for a position in their organization. She went. However, during the interviewing process, when it became known that her internal Soviet passport[4] contained the notation "Jew," the institute had immediately dismissed her.

Trying to prepare me for the worst, Mother warned me that I must realize that not every institution would accept me, because of one word written with indelible ink on my passport—Jew.

But Gorbachev's words had given me hope. With this new,

honest leader turning us back to the ideals of Lenin, anti-Semitism would be a thing of the past. I could go anywhere I wanted and climb to the highest stars. It was a brave new world, and I was ready to take off.

---

[1] The Western title of "Mr." is a deliberate insult. It says that I was not really a true Soviet citizen.

[2] The Great Patriotic War is how Soviets refer to World War II, as they view the war more as a defense of their homeland against Fascism rather than as a worldwide conflagration. Furthermore, they view themselves as the sole victors of this war.

[3] At the time (1985), one Russian ruble was equivalent to one U.S. dollar, as figured by the Soviet government.

[4] Every Soviet citizen was required to have an internal passport that serves as the main identification document for the person. Among all other information the passport lists the person's ethnicity.

CHAPTER 6

It was a hot and muggy July day in Moscow when I first saw MIPHE in 1988. At least it *seemed* muggy—I wasn't sure if it was just the weather or my sweaty palms.

The institute looked imposing, with a high wall surrounding the sprawling grounds and various structures that made up a combination of MIPHE and other "special" scientific government buildings.

After passing a special security checkpoint, I received a temporary restricted-access pass and lined up with 4,000 other hopeful candidates to receive an official application form. Four applicants vied for every vacancy.

The questions on the application form were straightforward. "How many years have you been a Komsomol member?" I wrote "3 years." "Have you ever been abroad?" "No." "Do you have relatives living abroad?" "No." "During the Great Patriotic War [World War II], did any of your relatives live in German-occupied territory?" "No." "Were any of your relatives taken captive by the Germans during the Great Patriotic War?" "No." "Have you or any of your relatives ever been in prison?" "No." So far so good.

Then came the final question: "What is your nationality?" Remembering the promises and plans of Gorbachev, I swallowed my fears and wrote "Jewish."

That was it for the first day of the long two-week process of trying to become a student at MIPHE. The remainder of the time I would spend studying for and taking three entrance exams—mathematics, Russian language, and physics. Every applicant received a useful booklet, *Help for New Students*. It contained sample problems and questions from MIPHE entrance exams of previous years.

Holding on tightly to the booklet, I caught a bus to another section of Moscow, where my aunt Esther lived. Aunt Esther's apartment was to be my home away from home while taking the entrance exams during the next two weeks. My father, who had come to Moscow on business, was also staying with Aunt Esther.

I had four days in which to prepare for my first exam, a mathematics test. Carefully studying my *Help for New Students* booklet, I analyzed and solved each problem in the math section.

Four days later I felt fully prepared as I walked into a large auditorium, where I, along with 300 other prospective students, would take the written exam. The test, which lasted three hours, was not too difficult, and I felt that I had done my best. Two days later the center posted all of the test grades, along with our names. Happily, I noted that I had received a 5.* However, 50 out of the 300 students had failed the exam and left the application process.

I was scheduled to take my Russian language/literature examination five days after the math exam. Again I turned to my *Help for New Students* and felt that I was as fully prepared as possible. It was another written exam, covering comprehension, grammar, and writing ability. Since I was from the Ukraine, I did not have to take the same exam that native Russian applicants were expected to complete, so I was not too worried about it. When the grades were posted, I noticed that I had received a 4, but 30 people had failed this exam and had to drop out. Our group was being whittled down, and I was glad that the physics exam was next.

Physics was the star in my crown. My favorite subject, I had been preparing for it all those years with Vef, my high school physics teacher. Having participated in six major Physics Olympiads, I was comfortable solving difficult physics problems during a limited time period in a tense, competitive environment. Furthermore, I was sure that I would at least get a 4 and probably a 5 on this exam, which would place my cumulative entrance exam grade well above 12, which was what I needed in order to be accepted into the institute. Brushing up with the questions found in *Help for New Students*, I eagerly waited for the examination day to arrive.

A few days later I walked into the large auditorium where I would take the physics exam. This test was different from the first two, as it combined both oral and written work. Upon entering the room, I was handed a sheet of paper with a physics problem to solve and two theoretical questions to answer. I had 40 minutes to analyze and solve the problem and to answer the other two questions. Then I was to present the paper to the examining professor, who would look at my work and ask follow-up questions.

After receiving my paper, I sat down and took a look at the problem: "Find the connection between the acceleration of the particle and its velocity and the tension of the electric and magnetic field."

Relieved that the problem was so simple, I quickly set about solving it. In less than 40 minutes I had completed the entire written portion of the exam, so I went to the front and handed my paper to the examiner.

The professor took the paper out of my hands and put it in a folder without even looking at it. Didn't he even want to check my work? Then, turning to me, he asked, "Determine the frequencies of the oscillations of a charged spatial oscillator that is located in an unchangeable consistent magnetic field; the frequency of the oscillator without a magnetic field equals *w*."

I was shocked. The problem was three times harder than the original written one, and I had not expected to receive such a difficult question orally, and with no time to prepare. However, I recognized it as one that I had encountered at the Physics Olympiads and was happy that I had studied the particular problem in a special physics book. Remembering how the book's author had solved this problem, I followed the same process and came up with the right results. Relieved, I thought this would satisfy my examiner and he would release me. Unhappily, it did not.

My correct answer to the difficult problem brought no reaction from the professor. Instead, it brought more misery as he gave me another problem as difficult as the one I had just solved. *What is going on?* I wondered. Why wasn't he satisfied with the first two problems I had already solved? Wearily, I picked up my pen and began solving the third problem. I was sure that I was following the right steps in solving it, but while trying to determine the correct integral I must have made a mistake, because when I arrived at the answer the coefficient was slightly off.

The professor slammed his hand down on the desk. "That's not correct!" he yelled. "You don't know anything! Be happy I'm giving you a 3!" There was nothing I could do about it. Leaving the room, I felt sick.

Out in the corridor I saw Alexei, one of my high school classmates. Just having completed his physics exam in an adjacent auditorium, Alexei looked relieved and happy. "It was easy," he said, describing the same written problem that I had been given at the beginning of the exam. "The professor just looked at the work I had done, asked me a couple of clarifying questions, and that was it." Alexei smiled and added, "He gave me a 5."

By now I began to realize that something was going terribly wrong, that someone, somewhere, was trying to eliminate me from the application process. Trying to swallow my growing fears, I climbed onto the bus and headed home to Aunt Esther's apartment.

Now I could do nothing but wait. Wait for the authorities to determine what the passing cumulative grade would be. With a 5 in math, 4 in Russian, and 3 in physics, I hoped the passing grade would be no higher than 12. Then I would still have a chance.

Two days later 12 was posted as the passing grade. I breathed easier. The next day I went back to MIPHE with a letter from Aunt Esther stating that I would not need space in the dormitory, because I could live with her. Since dormitory space was limited, I had been told that such a letter would help seal the decision to accept me.

I headed up the steps and into the main hall of the central building of MIPHE. Posted there on the bulletin board were the names of all those who had achieved a cumulative grade of 12 or higher. I fully expected my name to be there as I glanced at the list. But it wasn't. Carefully reading through the list again, I saw clearly that "Bolotnikov, Alexander" was not there.

With fear nearly exploding from my chest I headed to the registrar's office, where I explained the problem. "Something is really wrong," the registrar said with a concerned look on her face. "Everyone who had a cumulative score of 12 was accepted. In fact, even three people with a score of 11 made the list, so if your score was 12, you certainly should be on it." But as kind as she was, the registrar could do nothing to help me. My father would have to visit the rector of the institute, Grigory Sergeiovich Sholnov, to find out what the problem was.

The next day I waited nervously downstairs in the main hall

while my father went up one floor to the rector's office. After being cleared by the secretary to enter, Father waited patiently while Grigory Sergeiovich nervously straightened papers on his desk. Slowly looking up, he motioned to my father to take a seat.

"*Slushiyu* ["I'm listening"]," the rector said, so my father began.

"My son has passed all of the entrance examinations and achieved a passing cumulative score. He would not need dormitory space, because he could live with my sister here in Moscow. We have never had any relatives who have lived outside of the Soviet Union. Our family has always worked in atomic energy, and I am the vice-director of atomic power station construction in the Ukraine. I have a letter from our organization that states that a graduate from MIPHE is very much needed and that my son will be employed as soon as he has completed his coursework. What is the problem?"

Grigory Sergeiovich looked up from his desk. "You know," he began, "even though your son has reached the passing cumulative grade point and has a place to live, and even though we value all of your important letters and the important work you are doing in atomic energy, there were special decisions that we had to make about certain applicants." Pausing momentarily, he looked for a reaction. My father gave none. "You see, your son was not the only one rejected. There were four others who, even though they had passing grades, were rejected because of special circumstances. I have the list here," he said as he began reading names: "Epelbaum, Finkelstein, Frankl, Shwartz, and Bolotnikov."

It was obvious that all names except "Bolotnikov" had something in common—a definite Jewish sound. The only reason my last name differed was that my grandparents had changed theirs during the time of the Russian Revolution.

Now my father knew what the problem was. He had suspected anti-Semitism but had dared to hope otherwise. "I'm sorry," the rector said, "but this is the final decision of the admissions committee. There is nothing we can do about it."

As I watched my father come down the steps from the rector's office, I knew immediately that the visit's outcome had not been favorable. Father shook his head, and we silently walked together to the bus stop in front of MIPHE.

It was a long ride home that day to Aunt Esther's, but strangely enough, I still had hope. My belief in perestroika, glasnost, and Mikhail Gorbachev was still very strong. We still had one place of appeal—the Soviet minister of energy. My father would see his last contact tomorrow.

By 4:30 the next morning the sun was already shining over Moscow. A few hours later my father was on his way to see one of the highest-ranking government officials in the Union of Soviet Socialist Republics—the minister of energy.

The minister greeted my father warmly as he entered the office. They had known each other for several years and were good friends. "Well, what can I do for you, Vladimir Iosifovich?"

"There seems to be some kind of problem over at MIPHE," my father began. "My son, Alexander, has been preparing for years to enter MIPHE and has just completed the entrance exams. He has passed all of the exams, and his cumulative score was higher than the minimum needed for acceptance. However, his name did not appear on the list of those who passed. In fact, applicants whose scores were lower than my son's were accepted."

The minister looked puzzled. "Something is really wrong," he said. "I'm going to call Grigory Sergeiovich and find out what the problem is. I am sure there must be some mistake." Picking up the telephone, the minister called the rector at MIPHE.

"Hello, Grigory Sergeiovich? This is Mikhail Yuriavich. I have a question for you." My father listened intently as the minister asked about my situation. Then came a long pause as Mikhail

Yuriavich listened to the response on the other end of the telephone. As he did so, the official's face clouded over and a frown appeared. "Oh, I see," he said. After hanging up the phone, the minister turned to my father, who already knew the answer. "I'm sorry," Mikhail Yuriavich said, "but there's nothing that can be done. Your son will not be able to study at MIPHE."

One look at my father's sad, desperate face told me the answer. It was over—all the years of working, hoping, struggling with the system, believing that I would be accepted if only we got back to Lenin's basic principles. No longer was I a true believer.

As I threw aside all that I had learned and believed, a new thought came to mind: *If I'm a Jew, then I might as well find out why it is that so many people hate me.* With a new determination in my heart I walked down the street and caught the next trolley headed for an old Jewish synagogue located in the heart of Moscow. Perhaps there my questions would find answers.

---

*The Soviet grading system is a numerical system: 5 is equal to an A, 4 to a B, and 3 to a C. The number 2 is equivalent to an F. A 1 is never used, because it is considered too humiliating to the student.

CHAPTER 7

Tucked away on a shady side street just a stone's throw from the infamous KGB headquarters on Dzerzhinsky Square is the old Moscow synagogue. I had learned that my father's cousin was a rabbi and hoped to find him at the synagogue.

As I walked up the front steps of the old building, a dark-haired middle-aged man wearing a yarmulke, the traditional small cap that all male Jews are required to wear while in the synagogue, greeted me. Standing by one of the large pillars at the entrance of the synagogue, he handed me a yarmulke. It was clear that I was to put the little hat on before entering the building.

Guiding me around the corner and through another set of doors, the man led me right into another world. Quietly slipping into a side row, I watched as a small group of men recited the Wednesday noon prayer. Wearing prayer shawls and yarmulkes, they stood on the main level of the room, reciting traditional prayers and bowing at the appropriate times. Women watched from the open balcony lining both sides of the high-roofed chamber.

Flashing from the front wall was a huge golden mosaic showing an 18-foot Adam on the left, a 15-foot Eve on the right, with a 20-foot tree of life in the center. Mysterious writings in strange letters made a golden arc over the mosaic.

Silently I stood, absorbing the atmosphere. The songs, readings, prayers, artwork, and even the architecture of the building itself convinced me that here was something really ancient. For the first time in my life I realized that I had roots that reached far beyond the 1,000-year history of Russia.

In Soviet history classes we had talked about the ancient civilizations of Egypt, Phoenicia, and Babylon, but the word "Israel" never appeared in our textbooks or lectures. "Who are the Jews?" I had asked my uncle Alex when I was 10 years old. Uncle Alex was a designer of atomic submarines. He shared what he knew about the history of the Jews with me.

"A long, long time ago," he began, "there were two Jewish kingdoms—Judea and Israel. And these kingdoms were very ancient. They were well-developed civilizations and existed until the time of Rome. But then the Romans occupied their land, and the Jews began to leave Palestine. During the tenth century there were the Crusades. Palestine was the main battleground between the Christian crusaders and the Muslims. Since that time all the Jews are scattered throughout various countries of the world." That was all he could tell me.

But as I watched this Wednesday afternoon prayer service in the Moscow synagogue, I realized there had to be more to learn. I knew it was something much older than any Slavic culture, and I felt a great longing to learn about the deep and rich culture of my ancestors.

But how? Since nothing was written about Jewish history in any

Soviet books, I didn't know where to get more information. As I was leaving the synagogue, I noticed a tiny bookshop in the building's outside wall. Delighted, I quickly went to the window, where I noticed one book for sale—*Teachings of the Fathers.* It contained portions of the Jewish Talmud, a collection of rabbinical teachings formed during the second century out of the oral tradition. Quickly purchasing the book, I slipped it into my coat pocket and headed past the KGB headquarters to my aunt Esther's apartment.

That night my father and I went to Kievsky Vauxhall, where we caught a train going south to the Ukraine. But I was taking much more than just a train journey that night as I opened my new book and started to read. I was also on a spiritual voyage with a destination as yet unknown.

CHAPTER 8

I quickly devoured *Teachings of the Fathers,* the book I had purchased at the synagogue in Moscow. While I found a lot of wise teachings in it, I still had many unanswered questions, particularly about the Jewish culture. I felt like an adopted child who had just found his biological parents, and I wanted to know about my family history—all 4,000 years of it!

Classical Russian literature was of little help to me. Great Russian literature rarely mentions Jewish people, and when it does, the authors use the derogatory name of "kike"—such as "Kike Yankel" by Nicholai Gogol. Fyodor Dostoyevsky and Ivan Turgenev, two other great Russian writers of the nineteenth century, also refer to Jews as kikes in their writings.

One day as I was searching my parents' library for something that would enlighten me, I came across an interesting-looking three-volume set titled *Jewish War.* Leon Faichtwanger, a German Jew, had written the historical novel. In it I learned for the first time about the destruction of Jerusalem in A.D. 70. Fascinated, I continued reading as the author unfolded further events between the Jews, Romans, and Christians. The novel made a profound impact on me, because for the first time in my life I could see that anti-Semitism did not originate with Communism, but actually began centuries earlier and was developed further by the Christian church.

I learned more about how the Christian church encouraged anti-Semitism when I read another book by Faichtwanger—*A Jew by the Name Zuss.* In it I discovered that the Roman Catholic Church organized and encouraged all of Europe to participate in the Crusades in Palestine during the Middle Ages. "We must go and get the tomb of our Lord out of the hands of nonbelievers!" Pope Urban II commanded. His decree included attractive incentives of wealth, nobility, and fame to all brave warriors who would participate in the bloody massacre of hundreds of thousands of Jewish men, women, and children throughout the twelfth and thirteenth centuries.

Another interesting discovery I made in it was Kabbalah—Jewish mysticism. Kabbalah especially piqued my interest because a wave of mystical philosophy and spiritism was currently washing over the Soviet Union, and I was intrigued to discover that spirituality was also present in Jewish culture.

The more I read, the more captivated I became. I decided that I must go to the synagogue in Kiev and find out more about Kabbalah as well as some of the other teachings of Judaism.

However, when I shared my plans with my 88-year-old great-aunt Berta, she was terrified. "Sasha, please don't do that!" she pleaded. "I know you hate Communism, and I don't try to force my Communist views onto you, but I'm telling you that to go to the synagogue is really dangerous—don't do it. I'm afraid of pogroms."

I didn't understand what she meant, but I could see real fear on Aunt Berta's face. *Why would it be so terrible if I visited the synagogue?* I wondered. So I approached my mother. "Mama, why is Aunt Berta so afraid of my visiting the synagogue in Kiev? Aren't we Jews?" My mother also thought that going to the synagogue might not be a good idea, but at least she didn't express the terror that Aunt Berta had shown.

Aunt Berta was the last surviving member of her generation. Her sister Clara, who was my grandmother, had died eight years earlier. Her other sister, Sonia, was also dead. Eighty-eight years old, Aunt Berta had seen a lot in her lifetime, and my mother was sure that there must be some good reasons Aunt Berta was so afraid of my visiting a synagogue. Finally she decided to approach Aunt Berta about it.

"*Toyta*[1] Berta," Mother began, "why is it that you are so afraid of Sasha going to the synagogue? You know he's young and is just interested in learning more about his past."

"*Lyudichka,*"[2] Aunt Berta replied, "you need to know something about our family that you have not known before. My birth certificate, your mother's birth certificate, and Aunt Sonia's birth certificate were all forgeries." This was shocking news, because to have forged legal documents was a criminal offense.

Aunt Berta continued. "We were not born in Kremenchuk, Ukraine, and our father was not killed by anti-Semites during the Russian civil war, as stated in our documents. We were born in Israel." Her words hung silently in the air. What could my mother say?

Aunt Berta explained further. "Your mother and I and Aunt Sonia were all very young when our father and grandfather were killed in an Arab riot against the Jews in Palestine. It was sometime around 1907. Our mother didn't know what to do, so she brought us to the Ukraine, because her father and many other relatives were there. No one living, except for me, knows this.

"Ever since coming here from Israel, we have been afraid to go to the synagogue. We feared to do anything that identified us as Jews. Afraid of pogroms, we never went to the synagogue."

But there was much more to the story, as my mother and I soon discovered. Soon after her talk with Aunt Berta, my mother learned through her brother Alex that she had a 92-year-old uncle, named Laib, living in Moscow. Uncle Laib was the older brother of my mother's father. His existence shocked both of us, since neither Dedushka, Babushka, or Aunt Berta had ever mentioned him.

"I'm dying to meet this uncle," my mother said, "and I'd be happy if you'd go to Moscow with me to meet him." Of course I was interested, and a couple weeks later I found myself entering the Moscow apartment of this mysterious great-uncle.

Uncle Laib was really short—at about five feet—and quite husky. The 92-year-old man had been a geology professor at Moscow State University for many years and was still mentally sharp.

My mother talked with Uncle Laib for a while and told him about Dedushka's final years. After listening for a time, Uncle Laib asked, "And how is my cousin Clara doing?" Both Mother and I could hardly believe our ears. My mother's parents were cousins? We had certainly never heard that before. "Well, Mama died eight years ago," my mother said.

As Uncle Laib and Mother continued talking, much of the conversation was a mystery to me. I longed for the visit to end so that I could ask my mother all sorts of questions. After about two hours we left.

"Why did he call Babushka his cousin?" I asked as soon as we stepped outside.

"Well," my mother replied, "I don't understand a lot of it, but I do believe him about Babushka and Dedushka being cousins. It seems that our family came from a large and wealthy rabbinical clan that has lived in Kremenchuk for centuries. People were encouraged to marry within the clan, so Babushka and Dedushka married each other, since they were both part of this rabbinical clan."

"*Rabbinical* clan?" I asked. I was shocked, because it meant that our family had included rabbis for centuries, since it was an inherited position.

"Yes," Mother replied. "In fact, as the eldest son in his family, Uncle Laib used to be a rabbi. . . . And his father, and *his* father, and so on for centuries!"

"So what happened?"

"Well, Uncle Laib became the rabbi in Kremenchuk after his father died. In 1917, during the Bolshevik Revolution, he and his brothers, including Dedushka, decided they should quit believing in God, so Uncle Laib closed the synagogue in Kremenchuk. It ended family traditions that had existed for centuries.

"Uncle Laib came to Moscow State University, where he completed a Ph.D. in geology, and Yakov, your dedushka, began working for the KGB. But in order for Dedushka to work for the KGB, he had to cover up his strong Jewish past, especially the fact that he came from a rabbinical family and that his wife was born in Israel. That's why the birth certificates were forged."

"But why didn't Dedushka ever tell us about Uncle Laib?" I asked.

"I wondered about that too," Mother replied, "so I asked Uncle Laib why he and Dedushka never communicated with each other. It's a sad story.

"After completing his Ph.D., Uncle Laib moved back to Kremenchuk with his family. He and his wife had two children. Your grandfather and grandmother were still living in Kremenchuk at the time, where Dedushka served the KGB.

"Then when Hitler's Fascist troops invaded the Ukraine in 1941, they headed straight for Kremenchuk, which had been known as a Jewish settlement since the eighteenth century, when the czars forced all Jews across Russia and Ukraine into little settlements.

"Of course, with news of the Nazi troop invasion, everyone in Kremenchuk panicked as they tried to cram onto the last trains headed away from the invading troops. Because of his high rank in the KGB, Dedushka was able to secure places on the train for himself, Babushka, and my older brother, Uncle Alex, who was 14 years old. So our family survived.

"However, Uncle Laib was away in the army at the time, so his family was alone in Kremenchuk. Unfortunately, Dedushka wasn't able to help Uncle Laib's family escape—his wife and two children died in German concentration camps. Uncle Laib never forgave my father for this, and they never spoke to each other again."

It was a quiet trip back to Kiev, as both Mother and I were absorbed in our own thoughts. I remembered Dedushka's last years as he spent day after day just lying on his bed in our apartment. I wondered if he had been thinking about the dark secrets that Mother and I had only just discovered.

Growing up in an atheistic Communist family, I never dreamed that our family had been such an integral part of Jewish culture and religion for centuries. I had read about rabbis and other Jewish religious teachers in the books by Faichtwanger, but I had no idea that I was reading my own family history! Now I knew that my great-uncle had been a rabbi, and his father, who was my great-grandfather, and my great-great-grandfather, and so on back for several centuries. But who was I? The Communists didn't accept me. I wasn't considered to be Ukrainian or Russian. My passport was stamped "Jew," but I hardly understood what it meant to be Jewish. "If they say I'm Jewish," I decided, "I have to be *really* Jewish, not just on papers, but in reality."

So it was settled. No matter what Aunt Berta or anyone else thought, I simply *had* to visit the synagogue in Kiev, no matter what might happen.

---

[1] *Toyta* is the Russian word for "aunt."
[2] *Lyudichka* is a familiar form of the name "Lyudmilla" or "Lyuda."

CHAPTER 9

BE NOT LIKE
SERVANTS WHO
SERVE THEIR MASTER
FOR THE SAKE OF
RECEIVING A REWARD;
INSTEAD
BE LIKE SERVANTS WHO
SERVE THEIR MASTER
NOT FOR THE SAKE
OF RECEIVING
A REWARD.
AND LET THE AWE
OF HEAVEN
BE UPON YOU.

—*Avos 1:3*

A few weeks later I boarded a train headed for Kiev, greatly anticipating my visit to the synagogue. In addition, I planned to get some information from Kiev State University, at which I hoped to study that fall. Also, I wanted to see some friends and have time for a little fun.

Shortly after arriving in Kiev, I went to a downtown ticket outlet to find out what was happening in the evenings. As I scanned the posters advertising various theater performances and concerts, a most unusual ad caught my eye:

Rabbi Shlomo Carlibach
Jewish Music
Octyabrysky Palace of Culture
August 2, 1988
6:00 p.m.
Tickets: 2 rubles, 50 kopecks

I couldn't believe my good luck. Here I was in Kiev, just in time for a concert that would take place that very day! Eager to experience my first Jewish cultural event, I pulled out a five-ruble note and bought a ticket.

A few hours later I headed up the hill toward the Octyabrysky Palace of Culture in the center of Kiev. Approaching it, I noticed other individuals quickly but quietly approaching the building's entrance, hoping no one would stop and question them.

Kiev was known for its anti-Semitism, and the concert was the first-ever public Jewish event in Kiev. Posters advertising the concert had gone up all over the city, so it was no secret that a large number of Jews would be going to the Palace of Culture that Friday evening. I noticed that many of the men I had seen quietly walking up the hill had put on their yarmulkes as soon as they entered the building.

Walking upstairs to the first balcony, I found my seat on the front row. From there I had an excellent view of everything—the stage and orchestra pit, as well as the main floor of the concert hall. Never had I seen so many Jews—they filled the 1,000-seat hall nearly to capacity. I noticed several young people my age—in their late teens and early 20s—scattered throughout the auditorium, along with middle-aged and older people, all eagerly waiting for the concert to begin.

But it was to be much more than a concert. For nearly everyone present that night, it was to be our introduction to our roots, our first public affirmation of our rich and deep cultural heritage.

As the house lights dimmed, a middle-aged man with a full beard stepped onstage. He held a guitar, and I could see a small band behind him. The stage lights came on, and he began to speak in Hebrew, with a Russian translator by his side.

"Four thousand years ago there were great civilizations," he began. "The Moabites, the Babylonians, the Midianites, and the Jews. But today, where are these great civilizations? Where are the Moabites? the Babylonians? the Midianites? They are all gone. But where are the Jews? We are here tonight. After 4,000 years we are still here, and tonight I'm going to make Jews out of all of you."

Then beginning with the Exodus, Rabbi Shlomo Carlibach began to teach us our multimillennial history through music and word. "Through this day and night, He made us alive!" Rabbi Carlibach said, referring to the first Passover in Egypt. *Who is this "He"?* I wondered, *this "He" who made us alive?*

The rabbi plucked the introductory minor notes on his guitar, which were quickly joined by a consistent, syncopated beat on the snare drum and cymbals, followed by descriptions of God's deliverance of His people from all of their enemies down through history. Interwoven throughout the melody were several interesting and unusual sounds from the drums, cymbals, clarinet, and guitar. It was the first time I had ever heard such music, and it immediately entranced me.

The music, with its powerful words and strangely minor melodies interwoven with joyful praises, made a great impression on me. The songs continued to roll over me—"Glorious Is He"; "For From Zion Comes the Law"; "Rejoice!" The rabbi had wisely arranged the concert as a musical survey covering Jewish history and faith—the Exodus, God and His glory, the Torah, the future redemption of Jerusalem through the Messiah.

As I continued listening, some of my questions began to find answers. "God is keeping the Jewish people," Rabbi Carlibach explained. "He is to be glorified. We were in Egypt, and He saved us. In Babylon, and He saved us. All nations from that time have disappeared. But God has kept us alive, and we have remained a separate people among the nations for thousands of years. Glory and praise we are giving to His name."

As the music started again, the thought slowly began to dawn on me that here was more than culture, more than history. I began to realize that Jewish culture is blended with, and even based on, religion. The music I was listening to was not just folk music—the songs were about God. It appeared to me that God was in the center of Jewish thinking, and that it attributed all great historical events to Him. Jews even believed that it was God who had preserved the Jewish race and had kept them from assimilating! Here were totally new concepts for me.

As I sat there listening to the concert, my mind traveled back a couple years to the only other occasion I had seen people worshiping God. At that time it was quite difficult to find an active church anywhere in Russia, the Ukraine, or any other republic of the Soviet Union. However, my sister-in-law, Nadia, had really wanted to see the inside of an active Orthodox church, and I knew of one at Pokrovsky monastery in the center of Kiev. One Sunday morning when Nadia and I were in Kiev, we decided to visit the Orthodox church, so we got on a tram and headed for the city center.

Stepping off the tram at a stop not far from the cathedral, Nadia saw several beautiful bouquets of spring flowers for sale at a sidewalk stand and decided to buy a bunch.

Holding her flowers, Nadia quietly stepped into the dimly lit cathedral with me. Candles were burning everywhere, and the smell of melting wax mingled with smoke and incense permeated the place. Various icons with golden frames covered the high walls. A small group of worshipers, mostly babushkas, stood in the center of the huge room. The priest, dressed in rich robes with golden embroidery, had his back turned to us and was mumbling something in a low monotone that I couldn't understand.

Standing along one of the walls, we tried to be as inconspicuous as possible. However, we had already been observed, and soon a large man, dressed all in black and with a very long beard, approached us. I noticed a huge cross dangling on a heavy chain from around his neck. "Kikes! You kikes!" he screeched as he stared at Nadia's flowers. "How could you do this? Weren't you ever baptized?" He continued yelling as Nadia and I ran out the door, our hearts beating fast.

"Let's get out of here!" I said as we ran to catch the next tram headed away from the city center.

In my mind I now contrasted this somber memory with what was going on all around me at this concert. Rabbi Shlomo Carlibach strummed his guitar, slowly at first, as he sang. After a couple phrases the tempo picked up quickly, with the chorus and tambourines joining in. Soon everyone was clapping their hands with the strong rhythm of the song.

"All slaves have come out of Egypt and into Israel," sang the rabbi. "La la, la, la; la la, la, la—Je-ru-sa-a-lem, Je-ru-sa-a-lem!" The rabbi continued with an ever-increasing tempo. "Je-ru-sa-a-lem! Je-ru-sa-a-lem!" Again and again he repeated the phrase.

Then suddenly everything stopped. "Wait a minute!" the rabbi said. "What are you waiting for? Why are you so reluctant?" he asked while gesturing with his arms.

In a moment hundreds of us were on our feet. Several men from the rabbi's background chorus, dressed in *lopserdockst** and brimmed black hats, jumped from the stage to join us in our first Jewish dance.

Drawn by an irresistible urge, I left my balcony seat and, along with several other newly discovered Jews, headed downstairs to the main floor. Here was something that felt like "mine"—but it was also something unknown. In any case, I knew I needed to be there.

Quickly arriving on the darkened main level, I stood side by side with the others. Holding our arms out shoulder-to-shoulder, we grasped each other's arms and began moving sideways—like a giant merry-go-round. The music picked up again, and the rabbi started where he had left off. "They come from Egypt, and here they built a sanctuary, a temple. . . . Je-ru-sa-a-lem, Je-ru-sa-a-lem!" Faster and faster we went, round and round. I couldn't even see where my legs were going in the darkness, and I didn't care. Totally absorbed in the experience, I just kept looking up, listening to the music. "A temple . . . a sanctuary. . . . Jerusalem!"

Soon I began to feel that I was actually a part of this great nation with a long history—a nation that owes its existence and survival only to God, who kept us through the terrible years of persecution.

While dancing round and round with my fellow Jewish brothers, I couldn't help remembering the words of Vef, my favorite high school physics teacher. "You think that the Bible is a stupid book, but it appears that it really is not," he announced one day to the amazement of our physics class. "There are things that may not be so literally understood in the Bible, but one thing that I think is really clear is this: the world did not create itself. This belief has been held by many famous physicists, such as Isaac Newton, Albert Einstein, and many others."

Thinking of the words Vef had spoken just one year earlier, I realized how true they were and that the God who created the universe was not just an abstract Creator, but the God of the Jews!

During that dance in the dark I experienced a deep desire to learn more about this God, not only through the scientific evidences that I had discovered in physics class, but through an in-depth study of the Torah. I had only a blurry idea about the Torah, but I thought it spoke directly about God, and I longed to know more.

Slowly the music faded away and the dancing stopped. Everything was quiet. "It has been nice to be together," the rabbi concluded, "but now it is time to leave. This has been your first introduction to the Jewish culture, and I hope it won't be your last. I believe you will all want to come to synagogue and learn how to serve our Holy One, blessed be He."

Then another man came onstage. I guessed by his dress and confident manner that he must be a leader in the Jewish community of Kiev. "It is nice that the rabbi has invited you to come to synagogue," he said. "But unfortunately this evening we can't all go together, because the synagogue is already full of people waiting for the rabbi to conduct the Friday evening service." My heart sank. "But," the unidentified man continued, "you are all cordially invited to our Ninth Day of Ab service next week."

So the crowd left. As I wandered down the hill toward Ulitsa Kreschatik—the main street of Kiev—a black limousine suddenly appeared, driving right past me. Rabbi Shlomo Carlibach was inside, heading toward Podol, the city district where the synagogue was located.

Instantly I had an incredible desire to follow the rabbi and go to the synagogue that very evening. Quickly running to the nearby metro station, I ran down the steps and hopped on the first train headed north, hoping I would find the synagogue in time.

---

*The Yiddish name for the traditional long black coat worn by Russian Jews.

CHAPTER 10

LET THY HOUSE

BE A

MEETING PLACE

FOR SAGES;

SIT IN THE DUST

OF THEIR FEET;

AND DRINK

IN THEIR WORDS

THIRSTILY.

—*Avos 1:4*

While I had a great desire to reach the synagogue, I had only a fuzzy idea as to its exact location. I knew it was somewhere in Podol, but where? Afraid to ask anyone on the metro about the synagogue, I guessed at which stop I should get off.

Not knowing that I had stepped off the metro about two miles farther than I should have gone, I began wandering up and down the streets of this Jewish ghetto. Later I learned that in Yiddish this section of town was called "Yeagoupets," meaning "Egypt."

Jews had occupied the district for centuries, and once-stately homes bordered the tree-lined streets. When Communism came to power in Kiev, the authorities turned the large homes into communal houses, where dozens of families crammed together and lived in single tiny rooms.

The district was familiar to me, because it was where my family's friends Zechariah and Natasha lived. While they did not have to reside in one of the communal houses, Zechariah's mother did.

That evening, as I walked past dozens of these old communal houses looking for the synagogue, I remembered when Zechariah and I had visited his mother in her communal dwelling.

As we had approached the home where she lived, I had been impressed how old the house was. I had never seen such a big old house. Stepping inside, we found ourselves in the longest corridor I had ever seen, with 17 doors lining the dim hallway. After knocking on one of the mysterious doors, we entered a little room, 10' x 10'. Furniture crammed the room—a bed, wardrobe, round table, dish cabinet, and armchair, as well as a couple smaller chairs. We could hardly breathe, much less move around. It was fortunate that Zechariah's mother lived alone. Several other Jewish families of three or more people lived behind the other doors lining the hallway.

While Zechariah and his mother were visiting, I became increasingly uncomfortable. Finally I asked if I could use the toilet. Zechariah's mother led me out of the tiny room and back into the hallway. As she ushered me along the corridor, I wondered why she didn't just point out to me where the bathroom was located, rather than escorting me. However, when we reached the end of the corridor, I realized why an escort was necessary. Along the wall outside the bathroom door were 17 electric light switches. She showed me which switch was hers, so she would be charged for the use of the electric lightbulb rather than one of the other communal inhabitants.

Thanking her, I hoped that now she would leave—but she didn't. Opening the door, she motioned for me to step into the little room. Once inside, I saw 17 toilet seats hanging on the wall—and one toilet. She picked out the right seat and left me alone. During my time in the bathroom I noticed I was not alone. Cockroaches scurried across the floor, no doubt looking for something interesting to do. Such company inspired me to finish as quickly as possible. I put the toilet seat back on the wall and turned off the correct light switch.

Heading back down the dark corridor, I glanced into the communal kitchen. Inside were four gas stoves, each with four burners. Atop each burner was a pot of something cooking for one of many families. The mixture of the various odors made the room seem stifling. While I was glancing around, one of the residents came in, looking for the nice round loaf of Ukrainian bread he had bought earlier that day. To his distress, instead of finding the loaf, all he saw was big crumbs and chunks across the table. It was obvious to both of us that somewhere in that kitchen was a fat and happy rat!

I had never lived in such conditions and was happy to have grown up in a comfortable home in a small village rather than in a city ghetto. I was also glad that Zechariah and Natasha lived in better conditions, especially since my family visited them frequently.

But now here I was, a few years after my experience at Zechariah's mother's apartment, wandering the same neighborhood, passing the same old, rundown communal houses. Many of them were now almost empty because of perestroika and the emigration of thousands of Ukrainian Jews to Israel. However, not everyone had left, and in some windows I could see the light of Sabbath candles flickering in the growing darkness.

Determined to find the synagogue, I continued scanning the streets, searching for the Jewish house of worship. Late evening turned into dusk, and dusk to night. At last my eye caught a driveway with pillars and an iron gate in front. In the darkness I couldn't see exactly what was behind the gate, but it looked different than the other buildings. As I approached the gate, I could see words written on a metal sign: "Kiev Jewish Congregation." And beside it were interesting-looking letters: בית הכנסת קייב.

So this was the synagogue! Judging from the quiet darkness surrounding the place, I decided that the service was over. It was too late this time, but I determined that I'd be there for the special Ninth Day of Ab service the following week.

The next several days seemed to crawl by as I eagerly awaited the arrival of Friday evening. At last the moment came, and I again approached the gates with the mysterious Hebrew letters on them.

Following the others into the side door of the synagogue, I entered a small vestibule. As I headed for the main doors into the sanctuary, a quiet man about 60 years old met me. He was dressed in a long black coat with a prayer shawl and black hat. I assumed he was the rabbi, but later learned he was one of the cantors, a leader in the worship service.

As I approached the doors, he quietly said to me, "You are not allowed to go in there dressed like that." Wearing a dress shirt and trousers, I thought I had dressed acceptably, so his statement took me by surprise.

"Why?" I asked.

"You have to cover your head first," he said. It was a real problem—especially in the middle of August, when it's hot. I searched my pockets for some sort of cap or hat, but there was nothing. I knew that ideally I should wear a yarmulke, but they weren't handing them out on the steps, as at the Moscow synagogue. *Where in the world could I find a yarmulke?* I wondered.

I could hear the service beginning and longed to be inside the sanctuary. It had been a very long week as I had counted the days until I could attend, and now what a disappointment not to be able to go inside! As I was trying to figure out how in the world I could enter the sanctuary, the answer suddenly came bursting through the outside entrance doors.

The man was obviously headed straight for the sanctuary, but he didn't have a head covering either. However, just before stepping inside the sanctuary, he whipped a handkerchief out of his jeans pocket, draped it over his head, and walked in. It looked really crazy, but I immediately realized that if I was going to attend the service, that was what I would have to do. Feeling terribly embarrassed, I took a handkerchief out of my pocket, unfolded it, and placed it on top of my head. The cantor smiled and opened the door.

As my eyes adjusted to the dim lighting inside the sanctuary, my embarrassment instantly melted away. Among the 100 or so men sitting on the main floor, at least 50 of them were wearing handkerchiefs on their heads! The women worshipers, who were required to sit in the balcony, did not wear head coverings.

Taking a seat in the "handkerchief section," I listened as the cantor sang the liturgy. Even though everything was in Hebrew, I enjoyed the pleasant melody. Noticing that the person next to me was holding some kind of small prayer book, called a *siddur*, I edged closer to him, hoping to follow along. To my gratification the *siddur* contained a Russian translation of the service, and I tried to follow along as best I could in the quickly moving service. Watching those around me, I spoke when they spoke, bowed when they bowed, and sang when they sang. While some were responding in Russian, others were able to participate in Hebrew. Envying them, I wanted to be *really* Jewish and speak the tongue I had never learned. Unfortunately, I didn't know even a single letter of this interesting-looking language.

As the service continued, my longing to learn it grew stronger and stronger. "How could I learn Hebrew?" was the big question in my mind. The desire reached its peak at the end of the service, when the rabbi, who had been sitting, suddenly stood up and walked toward the front of the sanctuary. Approaching the wall, he reached behind a beautiful but mysterious blue velvet curtain, embroidered with gold.

I could feel excitement in the crowd of worshipers and wondered what the rabbi was getting from behind the curtain. When he turned around, I saw him holding a large scroll, with a blue velvet covering that matched the curtains. The rabbi kissed it and then slowly walked toward the waiting worshipers. *This must be the Torah!* I thought. I remembered reading about the Torah being in the form of a scroll.

As the rabbi walked down the aisle, some worshipers kissed the scroll; others stretched out their hands just to touch it. As I reached out my hand, my fingers skimmed the scroll's blue velvet cover as the rabbi passed by. It was exciting to actually touch these sacred writings! My desire to study the Torah deepened, and so did my longing to learn Hebrew, as I realized it was the only way for me to really understand the Torah.

After the rabbi had walked throughout the sanctuary holding the sacred scrolls, he returned them to their special place behind the blue velvet curtain. Meanwhile, the congregation sang the closing song. My spirits were so high I felt as though I could reach out and touch the clouds.

After leaving the sanctuary, I noticed a little book for sale—*Licutey Omarim Taniya* ("Collection of Speeches") by Rabbi Schneur Zalman from Lyady. I opened the book and noticed that on one side was Hebrew and on the other side a Russian translation. Buying the book, I hoped that it would help me understand the Torah as well as my past better. As I continued looking at the book, I noticed a piece of paper glued inside the back cover:

Jewish Cultural Society

Volodiya Donits, Chairman

(044) 229-23-59

That evening, when I returned to the apartment of our family friends, Zechariah and Natasha, I called the phone number, wondering what the "Jewish Cultural Society" was all about. A man answered the phone and courteously invited me to come to his apartment at 7:00 p.m. on Monday evening. I agreed immediately and counted the days until Monday. Fortunately, it was only two days away.

CHAPTER 11

ANYONE

WHO CONVERSES

EXCESSIVELY

WITH A WOMAN

CAUSES EVIL

TO HIMSELF,

NEGLECTS

TORAH STUDY,

AND WILL EVENTUALLY

INHERIT

GEHINNOM.

—*Avos 1:5*

At 7:00 p.m. the next Monday I stood at the door of Volodiya Donits. Walking into the apartment, I could see a group of Jewish people sitting in a circle and reading something—it was the Torah!

Taking a seat, I watched and listened intently as they read and discussed the sacred writings. Tears came into my eyes as I realized the helplessness of my situation—I longed to read the sacred Hebrew scroll and join in the discussion, but was totally unable to do so.

After class Volodiya came over to me and said, "Don't be disappointed. You need to find a Hebrew teacher. Here is a list of names from which to choose." He handed me a typed list of names and various locations where I could study Hebrew. Picking out the name of Naphtali Karabchievsky, I planned to begin Hebrew classes that very week.

Naphtali was a great man. I joined his three-month intensive Hebrew course. We met for two hours, three days a week—and the time flew by like seconds. I was like a thirsty man gulping gallons of cool water. In about three weeks I was able to read my first story completely in Hebrew:

"In the year 1099 C.E.[1] there were many Jews living in Jerusalem. The Jews lived together with Christians and Muslims. A few years after this the crusaders came. There was a great war, and many Jews were killed. Two centuries later Jerusalem was declared to be free of all Jews. However, in the year 1266 C.E. a great rabbi, named Mosheh Ben Nahkmann ('Rambam') came from Spain. He found two Jews living in Jerusalem, and he built a synagogue for them. Since that time a synagogue has always existed in Jerusalem, thanks to the synagogue of Rambam."[2]

The story gave me a lot to think about. The only thing I had heard about the Crusades was that the pope had commissioned Christians from across Europe to "reclaim" Christ's tomb from the hands of "nonbelievers." Sadly, I still had much more to learn about this tragic period of history. Nevertheless, I was ecstatic to be learning to read Hebrew.

One day Naphtali said to me, "There is a teacher from Israel who will instruct you to speak modern Hebrew." Before I could say anything, an elderly woman entered the room and said, *"Schme Esther. Mah-sham-hah?"* I tried to answer in Russian, but soon realized it was hopeless. Not knowing any Russian, only Hebrew, she kept repeating, *"Schme Esther. Mah-sham-hah?"* until I understood that she was introducing herself and wanted to know my name. *"Schme Sasha,"* I finally replied.

"Naim meod," she immediately answered. With great joy I realized that she understood me.

"Naim meod," I repeated. Thus began my journey into spoken Hebrew.

During the three-month intensive Hebrew course, I became

good friends with another student, Chaim. Chaim was a librarian at the yeshiva, the rabbinical school, and I enjoyed being around him. One day we went to the synagogue together, and he introduced me to many of the people, including Bension Moseiyevich, who worked at the front door greeting people and giving out information.

"Do you know what kind of mitzvah [law] a Jew must perform every day?" Bension asked me.

"No. What?" I responded. Then he pulled out two little black boxes attached to wide straps. Inside the boxes were tiny Hebrew scrolls with portions of the book of Deuteronomy written on them. "These are tefillin," Bension explained as he helped me strap one to my forehead, the other to my arm. Then he said a prayer and asked me to repeat it after him: *"Buruch attah Adonai elohaynu melech Haolam.* ["Blessed be Thou, Lord our God, the King of eternity, who sanctified us in your commandments and commanded us to put on the tefillin"]." It was my very first prayer.

Then Bension invited Chaim and me to join a lecture going on in the yeshiva downstairs. A *sofer,* or scribe, visiting from Israel, was explaining the whole process of making the tefillin. "The Talmud requires great dedication from scribes," he said, "because the writing must be perfect. Tefillin is like a radio transmitter through which you speak with God. If one detail is missing, it won't work. And if you make a mistake and do not correct it, it's a crime, because then a man thinks he's connected with God, but he really isn't!"

As I carefully studied the tiny Hebrew writing, I decided that it was a miracle anyone could write so small—especially perfectly! At the end of the lecture the yeshiva director invited everyone to a special Rosh Hashanah service the following evening. Chaim explained to me that Rosh Hashanah was not only the beginning of the Jewish new year, but also a serious time when we are to repent of our sins and prepare for the holiest day of the year—Yom

Kippur, the Day of Atonement—which follows Rosh Hashanah 10 days later.

The next evening as I approached the sanctuary doors, I pulled out my handkerchief and put it on my head. The cantor smiled and said, *"L'shana Tova Tikatevu* ["May you be inscribed for a good new year"]." I returned his smile and walked through the open door.

Joining the other worshipers in the "handkerchief section," I again followed the liturgy found in a little prayer book the person next to me was holding. This prayer book was slightly smaller than the one I had seen at the previous service. I later learned that the smaller book was a *mahzor*—a prayer book used for special holy days.

But what really captured my attention was the blowing of the shofar horn. Periodically throughout the service one of the cantors would stand and blow the ram's horn, making a loud, distinct sound. In between the blowing of the horn, a collection of special prayers was read. As I silently read the Russian translation of what the cantor was singing, my understanding and appreciation of this holy day grew deeper.

"Let us proclaim the sacred power of this day;
  It is awesome and full of dread.
  For on this day Your dominion is exalted,
  Your throne is established in steadfast love;
  There in truth You reign. . . .
  You open the book of our days,
  and what is written there proclaims itself,
  for it bears the signature of every human being. . . .
  As the shepherd seeks out his flock,
  and makes the sheep pass under his staff,
  so do You muster and number and consider every soul,
  setting the bounds of every creature's life,
  and decreeing its destiny.

On Rosh Hashanah it is written,
on Yom Kippur it is sealed:
How many shall pass on, how many shall come to be;
who shall live and who shall die. . . .
But repentance, prayer, and charity
temper judgment's severe decree.
This is Your glory; You are
slow to anger, ready to forgive.
Lord, it is not the death of sinners You seek,
but that they should turn from their ways and live. . . .
Man's origin is dust, and dust is his end.
Each of us is a shattered urn, grass that must wither,
a flower that will fade, a shadow moving on,
a cloud passing by,
a particle of dust floating on the wind,
a dream soon forgotten.
But You are the King, the everlasting God!"[3]

Again the shofar horn was blown, and the people responded by standing. The special service continued for several hours, but I was not tired. I felt that I was becoming more and more a part of the Jewish community.

I continued studying Hebrew in Naphtali's class with my friend Chaim, yet I still longed to study the Torah and teachings of the rabbis in a deeper way. Knowing of my desire, Chaim helped me enroll at the yeshiva, where I could learn more about the Talmud and Torah. The yeshiva held classes Sunday through Thursday from 6:00 to 10:00 p.m., and rabbis who had come from Israel taught them entirely in Hebrew. I was glad now for all the hard work I had put into Naphtali's and Esther's Hebrew classes, because the rabbis took for granted that we could understand Hebrew and did not spend much time on grammatical explanations.

My favorite place at the yeshiva was the library. It contained many interesting books that I intended to study, such as guides on how to read the Talmud and books on the history of Judaism. The history books were especially helpful in giving me a deeper understanding of what the rabbis were presenting in class.

The library also contained biographies of several well-known rabbis. One that especially interested me was the biography of Moses Maimonides, often called "Rambam" from his title of Rabbi and his initials (Rabbinu Moshe ben-Maymon), the greatest Jewish philosopher of the Middle Ages. From his biography I learned that Maimonides was not only a great philosopher but also a physician and one of the greatest Torah scholars of all time. He wrote a commentary on the Mishnah and an enumeration of the 613 mitzvoth (laws). In addition, he prepared a code of Jewish law and called it the *Mishneh Torah*, the commentary on Mishnah and Torah. Maimonides intended that a Jew would no longer have to struggle with the Talmud or rely on the unreliable opinion of his local rabbi—he could look into the *Mishneh Torah* and find the answer to every religious question he might have.

The great man's life story especially interested me as I read more about the trip Maimonides had taken to Jerusalem at the end of the Crusades.

Eyewitnesses told Maimonides terrible stories about the fate of the Jews who had lived in Jerusalem, including one particularly horrible instance when the Crusaders had killed so many Jews that blood flooded the city. But this was not enough for these murderers. They went house to house, searching for any Jews who might have been missed. At this time several Jews in the city who had converted to Christianity were trying to preserve some of the holy places, such as Golgotha and the Via Dolorosa. But in spite of the fact that they had converted to Christianity, the crusading "soldiers of Christ" dragged the innocent men, women, and children out of their homes and down the streets of Jerusalem to the synagogue. There they pushed them inside, along with a few remaining non-Christian Jews, and bolted the doors shut. Someone started a fire, and amid the screams of the victims inside, the "soldiers of Christ," led by a Catholic bishop holding a large crucifix, marched around the burning synagogue, proclaiming, "We avenge for the blood of Christ!"[4]

When Maimonides learned of the horrific events, he wrote a book titled *Moreh Nevukhim*—"Guide for the Perplexed." In it Maimonides tried to warn Jews against converting to Christianity in order to save themselves. "Christians will always remain the enemies of the Jews, and as long as you are a Jew, they will find you and kill you. The only hope is in expecting the Messiah,"[5] he declared.

In the *Mishneh Torah* Maimonides describes the coming of the Messiah. "The Jewish state will be restored and the Jews will return to Palestine. Then there will be a great war and at the climax of this war, Messiah will come and restore the temple."[6]

After reading Maimonides, I concluded that the main enemy of the Jews was the Christian church. I could see how the Christian church had persecuted them for centuries and that what had happened under the czars in Russia or Hitler in Germany was nothing new. Also, I began to understand why some Russian literature had such terrible things to say about Jews. For example, one author wrote that during the Middle Ages Jews needed the heart and blood of a Christian baby in order to celebrate Passover.

As I continued my historical reading, I found that the Orthodox Church was just as ruthless in its persecution of Jews as the Roman Catholic Church. Czar Nicholas I (1796-1855) developed a three-part plan to deal with the Jews in Russia. One third would be forced to emigrate, one third would be forced to convert to Russian Orthodoxy, and one third would be killed.[7]

Furthermore, I read that the Russian government encouraged anti-Jewish feeling among the peasants, hoping in this way to deflect the peasants' rebellious frustration and prevent a revolution. From time to time the czars would initiate a pogrom, which might begin in a village after an Orthodox priest, who was paid by the government, gave an anti-Jewish sermon in church. Paid agents would agitate against the Jews. Free liquor might be distributed in the village to encourage foolish bravery. In the pogrom some Jews would be beaten and some might be killed. The mobs would burn houses and destroy property. It was because of such terrible pogroms that my grandparents betrayed their religion and supported the Communists at the time of the Bolshevik Revolution in 1917.

Another book I came across in the yeshiva library was *Kuzary*, written by Jehudah Halevi, a rabbi from Spain. Kuzary is the name of a barbarian king who tried to find the truth between Judaism and Christianity. The book is basically a dialogue between the rabbi and the king. The king held the common Christian belief that the Old Testament was old, useless, and out of date, but that the New Testament was an important book. Attempting to show the beauty of the Old Testament to the king, the rabbi pointed to the book of Daniel, saying, "Look. We Jews know the future."[8]

This captured my attention immediately. Was it possible to know the future? I decided that I had to read the book of Daniel as soon as possible. The next day I went to the yeshiva library, sat down at a table with the sacred writings, and opened to the book of Daniel, hoping to gain at least a glimpse of what the future would bring.

---

[1] Common Era, a term used by Jews and others in place of the Christian A.D., or *Anno Domini*, "in the year of the Lord." B.C.E. is used rather than B.C., or "Before Christ."

[2] Solomonic, *Practical Grammar of the Modern Hebrew* (Jerusalem: 1983; published in Russian).

[3] A selection from the works of Rabbi Amnon of Mayence, from the translation found in *Gates of Repentance* (New York: CCAR, 1978).

[4] *The Biography of Rambam* (typewritten manuscript published in Russia, trans-

lated from Hebrew). Such books existed in the Soviet Union when the distribution of any religious literature was illegal.

⁵ *Moreh Nevukhim* (Jerusalem: Shamir, 1981; published in Russian).

⁶ *Mishneh Torah* (Jerusalem: Shamir, 1985; published in Russian).

⁷ Stephen M. Wylen, *Settings of Silver* (Mahwah, N.J.: Paulist Press, 1989), p. 242.

⁸ Jehudah Halevi, *Kuzary* (Jerusalem: Shamir, 1987; published in Russian).

CHAPTER 12

ACCEPT

A TEACHER

UPON YOURSELF;

ACQUIRE A FRIEND

FOR YOURSELF,

AND JUDGE

EVERYONE

FAVORABLY.

—*Avos 1:6*

The book of Daniel was like reading an interesting history book filled with exciting stories and strange dreams—a big metal image with a golden head, three Hebrews thrown into a fiery furnace and surviving, a king going crazy and eating grass, mysterious handwriting on the palace wall, and Daniel spending a night with lions and living to tell about it.

While they were great stories, nothing really struck me as vitally important until I read chapter 7, in which Daniel describes his strange dream. In his dream Daniel stands beside the sea and watches as four strange beasts come out of the water. The first is a lion with eagle's wings, but suddenly the wings get torn off. Then appears a bear, with one side higher than another and three ribs in its mouth. After the bear rises a leopard that has four heads, and four wings on its back. But the worst is yet to materialize. Suddenly a terrible beast roars out of the sea.

I felt as if I were on the seashore with Daniel as I read his description of the terrible beast in verses 7 and 8:

"There before me was a fourth beast—terrifying and frightening and very powerful. It had large iron teeth; it crushed and devoured its victims and trampled underfoot whatever was left. It was different from all the former beasts, and it had ten horns. While I was thinking about the horns, there before me was another horn, a little one, which came up among them; and three of the first horns were uprooted before it. This horn had eyes like the eyes of a man and a mouth that spoke boastfully" (NIV).

Wow! What a strange thing! I thought. The reference to the little horn especially puzzled me. *What is this thing?* I wondered. Then when I read verse 25, I found some clues to explain the little horn: "He will speak out against the Most High and wear down the saints of the Highest One, and he will intend to make alterations in times and in law" (NASB).

This is interesting, I thought. *The little horn has something to do with the "saints of the Highest One." Of course, the "saints of the Highest One" must be Jews. Who else would the Tanakh[1] call the "saints of the Highest One" except for the Jews?* I was sure that the verse was portraying anti-Semitism, but who was the leader of anti-Semitism portrayed as the little horn? I didn't have an answer.

For days and days I mulled the question over in my mind—*who is this little horn? Who is this person who has persecuted the Jews and has tried to change times and the law?* They were vital questions to me, since I had suffered from anti-Semitism during high school and in my outright rejection by MIPHE a year earlier. Since that time I had done a lot of reading about Jewish persecution in the Soviet Union and the history of the pogroms in czarist Russia. I often wondered how I could help my people stop suffering from anti-Semitism, but I knew the only escape was to emigrate to Israel.

It came as a real surprise to me that the book of Daniel seemed to predict anti-Semitism. It was also interesting that the mysterious little horn came out of the terrible fourth beast, which, as I discovered from my reading, represented the Roman Empire. From the things I had read in Faichtwanger, Josephus, and other authors, I knew that the Romans were the first to persecute the Jews methodically. *But who would come after the Romans?* I wondered. *Who is the one who continues persecuting the Jews—the saints of the Holy One?* The more I pondered these questions, the more important it was for me to find the answer to the riddle of the little horn. If I could only solve this puzzle, I reasoned, I would be able to find the root of anti-Semitism.

During the time I was pondering all these things, I continued to attend classes at the synagogue's yeshiva. However, I kept my questions about Daniel 7 and the little horn to myself, and just listened to the lectures. It so happened that it was now the celebration of Passover, or Pesach, one of the most holy days in the entire Jewish calendar, and the rabbi gave us a lecture about Pesach. He explained the history of the first Pesach, which Jews observed in Egypt on the night of their deliverance.

"The invisible God was showing His great omnipotence to the Egyptians," the rabbi explained. "He was punishing the Egyptians, but this was not His major purpose. His major purpose was to convince the Jewish people that even though He is invisible, He is still present. For generations the Jews had seen the Egyptians worshiping the various images of their gods, such as a frog, sheep, or bull, and many of the Jews actually took part in worshiping the images.

"The lamb that was to be eaten the night of the Pesach was actually one of the symbols of the Egyptian gods," the rabbi continued. "And God wanted to show that He was not contained in any image; and that this lamb was just meat and nothing else. We must remember this when we eat the Passover seder, and we must remember the miracles of the invisible Creator."

The rabbi's words made a big impression on me as I listened. "Every Jew is required to look upon himself as if he himself had participated in the Exodus from Egypt. . . . A Jew is one who identifies with the historical experience of the Jewish people. We might describe this as a sort of internal conversion, an inner spiritual experience of God's redeeming power achieved through the sacred ritual of the seder. One who does not share this experience may still formally be a Jew, but he is outside the community in any meaningful sense."[2] I realized the importance and solemnity of the holy day and wanted to share in the deeply meaningful and solemn experience of Passover.

A couple weeks after the celebration of Pesach I was in the center of Kiev and happened to notice a large crowd standing outside St. Vladimir's Cathedral. It was Easter Sunday for the Orthodox Church, and many of the people outside the cathedral were drunk. With slurred speech they gave each other the traditional Orthodox greeting: "Christ is risen!" "He is risen indeed!" came the garbled response. Old women clasped their freshly baked Pesach rolls, while others held their elaborately decorated Easter eggs. All were hoping to have their things sprinkled with holy water so they would be specially blessed. The whole scene made me sick.

Suddenly the thought popped into my mind about the little horn in Daniel 7 trying to change the holy days and the law. *Why do Christians celebrate the pagan holiday of Easter instead of Passover?* I wondered. After all, I knew that all of Christ's apostles had been Jewish. The rabbi had told us that they were traitors, but in the beginning they had all been Jews, including Paul. So if the founders of the Christian church were all Jewish, why did Christians celebrate the pagan rituals of Easter instead of the sacred services of the Passover? And why did they observe pagan Sunday instead of Sabbath?

In one of the many history books I had read I had come across an interesting letter written in the second century by the bishop of Antioch. He urged renouncing Jewish customs, which may have motivated the change of the holy day, Sabbath, to Sunday.[3]

In fact, the more I thought about it, the more I realized that the Christians had changed basically all holy days found in the Tanakh. I knew that the Tanakh, or Old Testament, as the Christians called it, was in their Bibles. Assuming that they knew what was written in it, I wondered why they didn't follow it.

"Who originated all these changes?" I asked myself. Probably the same person who started the Christian church. And of course everyone knew that it was the person called Jesus Christ. But if He was the founder of the Christian church, then He must have taught that the law and holy days needed to be changed. At that very moment Daniel 7:25 came to mind: "He will speak out against the Most High and wear down the saints of the Highest One, and he will intend to make alterations in times and in law" (NASB).

Could this be the key to unlock the mystery about the little horn of the terrible beast of Daniel 7? I wrestled with this shocking thought for about 15 minutes as I stood outside St. Vladimir's Cathedral watching the Easter rituals continue. *He "will intend to make alterations in times and in law,"* I thought. And His followers observe pagan Easter in place of the Passover. They keep pagan Sunday instead of the Sabbath. And of course, since He was the one who changed the law, then He was also behind all Jewish persecution and anti-Semitism, because the prophecy said He would "wear down the saints of the Highest One." My theory seemed to match history well, since the Jewish massacres during the Crusades were carried out by Roman Catholic Christians, and the Russian pogroms were the activity of the Russian Orthodox Church. The rabbi at the yeshiva had told us that the pope had strongly supported even Hitler's Holocaust.

I had no doubt as to the only sensible interpretation of Daniel's prophecy about the little horn. I felt excited and greatly relieved to have at last come to a solution of this puzzling mystery. Furthermore, I finally had the answer to the painful question regarding the origin of anti-Semitism. Now I knew what I had to do. I had to tell all the world that the little horn is the false Messiah, Jesus Christ! And most important, I had to inform the Jews that their main enemy was not the Communists or Hitler, but Jesus Christ.

---

[1] *Tanakh* is a Jewish term for what Christians call the Old Testament.

[2] Wylen, *Settings of Silver,* p. 134.

[3] Quoted in Samuele Bacchiocchi, *From Sabbath to Sunday* (Rome: The Pontifical Gregorian University Press, 1977), pp. 213, 214.

CHAPTER 13

OVER BABI YAR . . .

I AM FRIGHTENED.

TODAY I AM AS OLD AS THE

JEWISH RACE.

I SEEM TO MYSELF A JEW

AT THIS MOMENT.

I, WANDERING

IN EGYPT.

I, CRUCIFIED.

I, PERISHING. . . .

OVER BABI YAR

RUSTLE OF THE

WILD GRASS.

THE TREES LOOK

THREATENING,

LOOK LIKE JUDGES.

AND EVERYTHING

IS ONE SILENT CRY.

—*Yevgeny Yevtushenko**

One evening in September 1989 while I was attending yeshiva classes the rabbi announced, "Next week you are each invited to attend a special commemorative ceremony marking the forty-eighth anniversary of the tragedy at Babi Yar. Representatives from our government, as well as from Israel and the United States, will be present. We will have a special place of honor during the ceremony, and I hope that you will all plan to be there." Of course we all immediately agreed to be present at the important occasion.

While I had never been to Babi Yar, a small wooded valley with a sharp dropoff at the edge of Kiev, I had heard about the terrible things that had taken place there.

In September 1941, during the Nazi occupation of Kiev, the Germans had made a public announcement and had had posters put up all over Kiev instructing Jews to meet at Babi Yar. To ignore or disobey the command would be perilous. All Jews were expected to conform. The German authorities allowed them to bring as much luggage as they could carry. So on the morning of September 29, 1941, all across Kiev entire Jewish families—grandfathers and grandmothers, fathers and mothers, some pushing baby carriages, others holding their little ones in their arms while the older children helped carry luggage—made their way to Babi Yar.

As more and more Jews arrived at the little valley, the Nazis lined them up. The line of people stretched for five miles. Moving slowly along, the people went through various posts where they were forced to leave their belongings. At the first post they deposited their suitcases, then at the second post their coats and watches and jewelry, and on to the next post, and the next. Finally, wearing only their underwear, they reached their final point, where Nazi soldiers holding guns waited for them. Group by group the soldiers escorted their victims to the big cliff, where they shot them and threw them over. The massacre dragged on for two days, killing 100,000 Jewish men, women, and children.

And now, 48 years after the massacre, I was visiting the horrific site with the other yeshiva students. It was a solemn and moving experience. Looking up from where I was standing, I could see the powerful monument that had been erected in memory of those who had died. High on a cement slab ramp was a group of metal bodies twisted and dying together. What really caught my attention was the figure of a young mother, her hands tied behind her back but still trying to nurse her baby as she sat among the dead and dying figures. Unable to gaze at the monument any longer, I looked away.

Just then I felt someone gently brushing up against me and placing something in my hands. A second later the person was gone. Glancing down, I saw a book in my hands with the title *Habreet Ha Hadasha*. By this time I could translate the Hebrew words—"a new covenant," or "a new testament." Noticing that the book was written in modern Hebrew, I wondered what kind of new covenant it was talking about. However, I had no time to read it then, so I stuck it in my pocket, planning to look at it later.

The next evening at the yeshiva, the rabbi gathered all of the students together. "Yesterday a group of traitors were handing out books to you while you were standing at the ceremony. Who has this book with them?" he asked. We all stood up. "Please give them to me," he said. The students placed 20 or 25 books on the table in front of him. Quickly he grabbed all of the books and threw them into a burning fireplace. "That's what you should do when this book gets into your hands again!" he said. I realized then that the books must be the New Testament that Christians used. "We don't have anything to do with Christians!" the rabbi continued. "Let them go their own way. We're not trying to convert them to Judaism, and they should not try to convert us to Christianity! But every one of you should know," he said, looking around the room, "that after today if any of you ever willingly touch this cursed book, the blood of 6 million Jews killed by Hitler, as well as the blood of many millions more murdered during the Crusades and Inquisition, will be upon that person." It was a serious curse, and we determined then and there that we would never again touch this defiled book.

That fall, while still attending evening classes at the yeshiva, I enrolled as a physics major at Kiev State University. There I roomed with Igor Chaika, a close friend whom I had called "Chaika" ever since I met him at the age of 7.

Chaika was an intelligent person, talented in physics and mathematics. He also had two unusual hobbies that he had picked up while in high school—one was reading the Bible, the other listening to Western hard rock music. The Soviet Union banned both activities, but somehow Chaika got involved with them.

I remember the day he took me home with him and pulled out a rather worn old-looking book. It was a Bible. When Chaika opened it and started reading out loud, I was amazed to see that it was written in Old Slavonic text! *How can he read that?* I wondered. *It's so old and boring and difficult to read!* But in just a few months Igor read that old synodal Bible from cover to cover. I learned later that he had read it carefully and understood a lot of it.

Alexei, one of our high school classmates, introduced Chaika to his other hobby when he gave him a cassette tape of the rock group AC/DC as a birthday present. Soon Chaika also acquired tapes by the rock group Metallica.

Our dorm room at Kiev State seemed like a hard rock studio with pictures of AC/DC and Metallica covering the walls and Chaika's tapes continually blaring from his cassette player. Not only did he enjoy the music, but he enjoyed listening to the English words and trying to understand them. His knowledge of the Bible came in handy as he started recognizing several biblical motifs in the songs. "Listen to this!" Chaika said to me one day. "They are using words from the Bible, talking about Jesus Christ, but they are portraying him in a really negative way."

While I didn't really get into the music, I did like the words, as they reflected my understanding of who Jesus Christ was. I shared some of the things I had learned at the yeshiva from the Old Testament and explained my theory about Jesus Christ being the "little horn" described in Daniel 7. The more I listened to Chaika's music, the stronger my hatred became toward Jesus Christ.

One day Chaika introduced me to two of his friends, Ilya and Igor. Ilya was a poet, and the four of us enjoyed getting together to listen to Ilya's poetry, much of which dwelt on the theme of death. Ilya would read us his poems, and we would discuss many bizarre theories and tell him how great his poetry was and how he needed to publish it in a book someday. During one discussion I shared my hatred toward Jesus Christ and my theory about the "little horn" in Daniel. After hearing my theory, everyone agreed that

1973:

Two-year-old
Alexander, in Kremenchug

"Before and after"
pictures of the syna-
gogue in Kremenchug,
where Alexander's
great-grandfather,
Moses Alpin, was
a rabbi from
1880 to 1915.

1982: A group of Young Pioneers at the Pioneer camp near Moscow. (Alexander is in the first row, second from the right.)

1986: At the top of this eighth-grade class picture is Lenin as a baby. Immediately below Lenin is Vef, the physics teacher. In the second row (pictures one and three from the left) are Chaika and Alexander, who sat at the same desk at school for 10 years.

1986: Alexander (the tallest one in the picture) is among the graduates from the school of music in Kuznetsovsk. Communist posters in the background advertise the famous Twenty-seventh Congress, during which Gorbachev spoke.

1988: A school picture of Alexander and Chaika in Kuznetsovsk

Болотников Я.

Чайка И.

Березовец Я.

Alexander and this classmate made the inscription on the poster that got him into trouble.

1988: Alexander and his mother at the high school graduation in Kuznetsovsk

1988:
Alexander's
high school
graduation picture

Андрианов А.

1988: This classmate of Alexander's was accepted
into MIPHE in Moscow at the same time
Alexander was refused.

מיטגליד -בילעט‎ № ___653___				מיטגליד - אפיצאלן‎	
			יאר		
Болотников‎ פאמיליע‎			1989	—	
Александр‎ ג. אמען‎			1990	уплочено‎	
Владимирович‎ פאטער:‎			1991		
			1992		
			1993		
דאַס יאר פון אריינשרייטן‎			1994		
אלק דער געזעלשאפט‎			1995		
19 90 сент‎ " 16 "			1996		
			1997		
פאָרזיצער פון עם‎			1998		
געזעלשאפט‎			1999		
			2000		
19 90 сентябрь‎ " 16 "					

1989: The certificate of the member of the Society of Jewish Culture

1990: Alexander, with a group of student believers, at the time of his acceptance of Christ in the dormitory of Kiev State University

June 23, 1991: Alexander, with some of the 70 baptismal candidates at the baptism in the Dnieper River in Kiev

January 9, 1993: Wedding day for Alexander and Irina (shown with their parents)

1993: Alexander and Pastor
J. Robert Spangler at the
door of Kiev Catholic
Cathedral, where they
first met in 1991

1994: Pastor Spangler with
Alexander and Irina in a
Seventh-day Adventist church

1994: Alexander preaching in a
Seventh-day Adventist church

June 4, 1995:

Alexander and Irina on graduation day at Seminary Hall, Andrews University, Berrien Springs, Michigan

1995: Graduation!

1995:

Alexander and Irina Bolotnikov

1995: Alexander preaches at the General Conference session in Utrecht, Netherlands.

1995: In Jerusalem

June 1996: Alexander among the students of Zaokski Seminary extension school in Kiev (first row, fourth from right)

June 1996: The Dnieper River, in which Alexander was baptized

I had to meet a certain person named Grisha.

Soon afterward Ilya introduced me to Grisha, a guy with long hair and evil-looking eyes. "Grisha is a member of the Satan worshipers," Ilya explained. "You will find much in common with him, because he also hates Christ. His biggest desire is to go into St. Vladimir's Cathedral and do something that would defile it!"

Grisha and I talked together for several hours. I would tell him how much I hated Jesus Christ and the Christians, and he would explain how much he loved Satan. After listening to our conversation, Ilya and Igor gave me the nickname of "Judas," and soon I was known around Kiev among the groups of heavy metal listeners and Satan worshipers by that name.

Every once in a while the Satan worshipers would invite me to speak against Jesus Christ at their "church." They would say to me, "Judas, you know the Bible well. Tell us something from the Bible. What do you think of Jesus Christ?" While they sometimes read their satanic bibles, they never read the Old Testament for themselves, so were curious to find out what it said. I tried to explain some of the prophecies in Daniel, especially my theory about the little horn being Jesus Christ, but they didn't have enough education to understand my historical arguments. They mainly just wanted to hear me say negative things against Jesus Christ while they enjoyed their vodka. While I remained on friendly terms with them, I found that I didn't really have much in common with their group, made up mainly of uneducated drunks and criminals.

One day while we were sitting in the school cafeteria, Chaika asked me something that just about blew me out of my chair. "Judas," he said, "have you ever read the New Testament?"

"Never have and never will," I responded.

"Judas," he continued, "you're stupid. You may hate Jesus Christ as I do, but it doesn't mean you can't know anything about his life. It's actually very interesting. Besides, you should at least read the Sermon on the Mountain. It has a lot of wisdom in it."

"Come on, Chaika," I responded. "You know I'm Jewish. I can't touch that junk!"

Not one to be easily deterred, Chaika persisted. "If you can't read the New Testament because you're Jewish, and you believe that you can do only things that are acceptable for Jews, then you might as well tell us that you can't associate with us, because we're not Jews," he said, pointing to our friends around the table.

He had a point. I knew that technically I wasn't supposed to associate with non-Jews—the rabbis had taught us that at the synagogue—but somehow I viewed this as less serious than trying to read the New Testament. I was afraid of the curse the rabbi had pronounced upon anyone who deliberately took a New Testament in their hands after the experience at Babi Yar, and I didn't want to have the blood of millions of Jews upon my hands. On the other hand, I could see my inconsistency in not reading the New Testament and yet being so open with my non-Jewish friends.

"Come on, Judas," Chaika continued. "You know I'm not trying to convert you to Christianity. But this is so stupid of you to believe that if you know something about Christ you will betray your people. You don't have to believe and follow him; this stuff is just interesting to know. I never thought you were so rigid." I had a hard time believing that Chaika was being so serious about my reading the New Testament. I had known him for most of my life and had even sat with him at the same desk in school for 10 years, and never before had he been so insistent that I read anything. However, not wanting to lose his friendship, I finally agreed to look at the forbidden book.

---

*Excerpt from "Babi Yar," by Yevgeny Yevtushenko, from *Yevtushenko: Selected Poems,* trans. Robin Milner-Gulland and Peter Levi (Harmondsworth, England: Penguin, 1962), p. 82.

CHAPTER 14

SCHOLARS,

BE CAUTIOUS

WITH YOUR WORDS,

FOR YOU MAY INCUR

THE PENALTY OF EXILE

AND BE BANISHED

TO A PLACE

OF EVIL WATERS

[HERESY].

THE DISCIPLES

WHO FOLLOW

YOU THERE MAY DRINK

AND DIE,

AND CONSEQUENTLY

THE NAME

OF HEAVEN

WILL BE DESECRATED.

—AVOS 1:11

I opened the book and read the cover page:

НОВЫЙ ЗАВЕТ

ГОСПОДА НАШЕГО

ИИСУСА ХРИСТА

"The New Testament of Our Lord Jesus Christ." Turning the page, I wondered what I should read first. The Gospel of Matthew didn't look like something I wanted to get into, because I associated the word "Gospel" with the Orthodox liturgy, and I certainly wasn't interested in reading any liturgical literature. So I skipped over the four Gospels and came to a book called the Acts of the Apostles. *I certainly don't want to read about the acts of those traitors!* I thought to myself. *I know enough about them already!* Then came a bunch of letters by Paul, the arch traitor. *He sure wrote a lot of letters,* I thought as I thumbed through Romans, 1 and 2 Corinthians, Galatians, Ephesians, and so on. *What's so important about these letters that the Christians have included them in their Bible? It looks as though they really worship this Paul.* I could not help associating it with the 54 volumes of Lenin's writings.

As I continued riffling through the pages, I saw something that made me stop: the Letter to the Hebrews. To the Jews? How could this be? What could Christians possibly want to say to my people? Didn't they say enough to us during the Crusades? I just couldn't understand why the Christian New Testament would have a letter to the Jews. However, the temptation to see what Paul had written to the Hebrews was just too irresistible, so I started reading the letter.

Descriptions of Christ filled the first three chapters, and I viewed them as obnoxious appeals for me to believe in Christ. *What? Do they really want me to believe this stuff? And am I supposed to base this belief simply on their own words?*

I found Hebrews 3:7-9 especially irritating: "Therefore, just as the Holy Spirit says, 'Today if you hear His voice, do not harden your hearts as when they provoked Me, as in the day of trial in the wilderness, where your fathers tried Me by testing Me, and saw My works for forty years'" (NASB).

Man! I thought. *They're even trying to use the Exodus and events in the wilderness against me. I know the Jews had a problem in obeying God's voice in the wilderness, but these Christians don't have any right to tell me that this same voice of God is asking me to believe in Christ and that if I don't, then I'm hardening my heart, just as the Jews did when they were on the border of the Promised Land!* It irritated me that Paul tried to compare the ancient Israelites' disbelief with my refusal to believe in Christ as the true Messiah. I did not see any relationship between the two, and was angry that he was trying to draw a comparison.

However, in spite of my anger I kept on reading the book of Hebrews and found chapter 4 more puzzling than irritating. Verse 4 especially caught my attention: "For He has thus said somewhere concerning the seventh day, 'And God rested on the seventh day from all His works'" (NASB). That really confused me. How could a Christian Epistle use arguments based on the Sabbath? Furthermore, Paul didn't just quote the Torah (Gen. 2:2; Ex. 20:11), but in verse 9 he wrote: "There remains therefore a Sabbath rest for the people of God" (NASB). And of course, I knew that the "people of God" must be Jews.

Amazed, I was unable to solve this new riddle. Either the Letter to the Hebrews contradicted the rest of the New Testament, or else Christ and the New Testament writings did not forbid worship on the seventh-day Sabbath.

I remembered the rabbi telling us that Christian missionaries who give the New Testament to Jews want them to give up all of their beliefs and become non-Jews. But how could this book persuade me to forsake my Jewishness if in the Letter to the Hebrews it tells "the people of God" to continue keeping the Sabbath holy?

And even more puzzling was what Paul said at the end of chapter 4: "Since then we have a great high priest who has passed through the heavens, Jesus the Son of God, let us hold fast our confession" (verse 14, NASB). How could this be? I imagined that if Christ himself could hear Paul calling him a Jewish high priest, he would flip over in his grave! I thought that Christ was the enemy of the Jews, and to call him a *Jewish* high priest would be a great insult. And besides, what did Paul mean when he wrote "Let us hold fast our confession"? Paul was a Jew, writing to Jews. And isn't Judaism our confession? If that was so, then how did one relate it to the rabbis' opinion that the apostle Paul was the greatest traitor of the Jewish faith? If Paul was trying to change me from being Jewish, why would he tell me to continue observing the Sabbath and to hold fast my confession?

As I continued reading the Letter to the Hebrews, my eyes opened wider and wider. Throughout the letter Paul continued to unite Jesus Christ closer and closer to the Jewish Temple service. I couldn't reconcile the two. How could Jesus Christ fulfill so many roles in the Temple service? How could he, the enemy of the Jews, be our high priest? It seemed as though such perplexing questions and ideas were impossible to reconcile, and I did not know where to find the answers.

CHAPTER 15

BE AMONG

THE DISCIPLES

OF AARON,

LOVING PEACE

AND PURSUING

PEACE,

LOVING PEOPLE,

AND BRINGING

THEM CLOSER

TO THE TORAH.

—*Avos* 1:12

A couple months after Chaika had challenged me to read the New Testament, he came bursting into our dorm room at Kiev State with a mischievous smile on his face. "Judas," he said, "I have something interesting for you. I know you've met Orthodox Christians before, but what about the Pentecostals? Have you ever heard of such crazies?"

I remembered mention of them in a high school lecture given by Raisa Mikhailovna, a KGB officer who specialized in sects. She told us about a Pentecostal group that ate three children at one of their services in a village! I reminded Chaika of the lecture and asked if some Pentecostals lived in Kiev.

"Yes!" Chaika said excitedly. "And I've met one of them, and he doesn't look like a cannibal to me! Besides, he's a student here and lives in our dormitory, Room 623." I couldn't believe a cannibal was living so close. "As I understand it," he continued, "these Pentecostals are some type of Christian, so if you want to try out your theory about the little horn in Daniel 7, I think this is the field for you. A group of them are meeting at 5:00 in Room 421."

I glanced at my watch. It was five minutes to 5:00. I thought for a minute, then said, "Let's go." But as we were walking down the long hallway, getting closer to Room 421 with each step, my heart began sliding down to my ankles, and my pace slowed. Chaika hung back too. "Are you still in the mood to go?" I asked. He wasn't sure. It seemed as though we were both remembering Raisa Mikhailovna's lecture from five years earlier.

Unconsciously we headed back toward our room. After walking about 20 feet, we looked at each other, turned around, and headed straight to the cannibals' room. But after walking a few paces, we again reversed and went in the opposite direction. We went back and forth three times before Chaika finally said, "I'm sick of this! Do whatever you want, but I'm not going!"

So we went back to our room. I sat on my bed, mulling over the whole situation. "They're probably not eating children here in the dormitory," I reasoned. "And I'm big enough to fight them off, so they probably won't try to eat me!" I was terribly curious to see these strange people and learn more about them.

Finally I got out my talisman—a big silver Star of David on a silver chain—and put it around my neck, hoping it would bring me good luck. Having made my decision, I stood, walked down the hallway, and suddenly found myself in the cannibals' room.

It was a stuffy, crowded little room, and people were still coming in, finding places to sit on a bed or the floor. I sat on one of the beds near the back.

The meeting had already started, and one of the students was speaking. His name, I eventually learned, was Vanya, and I remembered meeting him briefly once before. He was excitedly repeating the name of Jesus. He kept saying it so much that it almost made me sick.

"Jesus loves you. He loves you as you are. He can forgive all of your sins. Even if they're very bad and very big." He kept repeating the phrases, and I didn't see any logic in them, just a lot of emotion. Finally Vanya ended his repetitious speech by making an appeal. "Well, whichever one of you wants to repent, even if you have repented before, let us pray and ask Jesus Christ for forgiveness."

It was terrible. Everyone else in the room knelt down on their knees, and I felt nauseated, because how in the world could I kneel before a liar and a false messiah? What did Vanya want me to do? To kneel and pray to the enemy of the Jewish people? I shivered just to imagine myself in such a position, so I sat where I was and didn't move.

The prayer was extremely long, and I thought it would never end. At last Vanya opened his eyes and saw me sitting there on the bed. His gaze focused on my Star of David. I noticed a spark of unhappiness in his eyes as he approached me and abruptly asked, "Brother, why didn't you pray?"

It was a good question, and I used it to start a discussion. "You asked me to pray to this Jesus, and you expected me to pray?" I said. "You might as well have asked me to pray to Satan and expected me to kneel!"

Poor Vanya was really shocked. "You don't understand," he said. "Jesus loves you. Jesus really loves you. Even if you have this," he declared, pointing his trembling finger at my Star of David, "He still loves you." Vanya's voice shook as he left the room.

Mixed feelings had struggled in me as I listened to him. On the one hand, it seemed that Vanya was really scared, but on the other hand he was telling me that Jesus loves me. It seemed that he was kind of forcing himself to say it, and I questioned his sincerity. I thought I knew everything about Jesus Christ. But I began wondering, *If Vanya's not sincere, why in the world is he saying, "Jesus loves you"?* His reaction to me was very different than that of the only other Christians I had met—the Orthodox Christians. As soon as they would see my Star of David or learn that I was a Jew, they would announce with all certainty that hell and all of its torments were expecting me and longing for my arrival. In their minds they saw no chance that Jesus Christ would love me, a Jew.

Why, then, was Vanya saying that Jesus loves me? I didn't understand. As I looked around the small room, I suddenly recognized another student—Nicholai, a second-year astronomy major, who lived in the village. I never would have expected that he would be among Christians, because just six months earlier I had seen him drunk and smoking cigarettes. I knew that Orthodox believers would drink and smoke, but people belonging to Christian "sects," as the Orthodox called Protestant groups, often did not drink or smoke.

As if he could read my thoughts, Nicholai said to me, "God has saved me. You remember that I was drinking and smoking just a few months ago, but with His power I was able to quit smoking in just two days." I appreciated the fact that Nicholai gave the credit to God rather than to Jesus. "And I haven't had a drink for five months already," he added. "I have a new life."

It was amazing. I compared Nicholai to Chaika and the Satan worshipers who drank every day. Personally, I didn't like to be drunk, and I hated to be around others who got drunk, so I really respected a person who stopped using alcohol.

"We have a lot in common," Nicholai continued. "Jews originated the Christian church. All of the apostles were Jews. Christ Himself was Jewish. And we respect and honor the Tanakh, which is in our Bible as the Old Testament."

"Yes," I replied. "I already know enough about Christianity, and I definitely know that Christ and his apostles were Jews, unfortunately. They betrayed the Jewish nation and preached idol worship, and you Christians kill Jews because we don't worship your idols.

"You are telling me that in your Bible you have all of our books, but they don't do you any good, because you were pagans and you remain pagans. You put images on your wall and then bow down to them, and because we don't do this, you call us 'Christ killers' and murder us!"

I was upset and could feel tension from the others in the room, but Nicholai remained calm. "I understand your anguish," he replied. "I know many Christians hate Jews, but I believe this hatred is from Satan. We are Protestants, and as you can see in this room, there are no icons."

I hadn't noticed this before, but as I looked around the room again, I could see that Nicholai was right. "We don't pray to any icons," he added. "We believe that God hears our prayers.

"Please don't be angry with Vanya. He is also a young Christian. But we are all sinners. If you want to know us and talk with us some more, you are always welcome here. No one will offend you. We have much in common, and we know that you understand a lot about the Old Testament. It would be interesting for us to learn more about it from you sometime."

They want to hear something from me? I thought to myself.

"Tomorrow our leader, Oleg, will be here," Nicholai said. "He is an experienced Christian—he has been in the faith for three years now. Oleg can probably tell you more about it than I can. I am sure you would enjoy talking with him and he with you."

As I headed back down the hallway toward my room, I was in shock. Protestants. I had read about them in my school history books. I remembered that Luther was against the pope, but that was about all I knew. But I didn't know that the Pentecostals, about whom the KGB told such crazy stories, were just

Protestants! The guys weren't cannibals—they were really nice! And they didn't seem anti-Semitic. Besides, Vanya even appeared to be a little bit afraid of me. I was probably too abrupt with him, I reasoned. And why would he say that Jesus loves me? The Orthodox believers would *never* admit that Jesus loves Jews! I remembered the frightening experience that my sister-in-law, Nadia, and I had gone through at Pokrovsky monastery when the man chased us out of the cathedral. There was no doubt in my mind about how the Russian Orthodox Church felt about Jews.

But these Protestants were really different from any Christians I had ever seen. No icons, no drinking, open and friendly, and they even invited me to join them again despite my hostile behavior! I decided that even though they said stupid things about Jesus Christ, they were still nice and I would come to their meeting the next evening.

Twenty-four hours later I was back in Room 421. Oleg, the "experienced" Christian, was 23 years old and had red hair. His speaking style was much different than that of Vanya. He didn't seem so hyper, and his words seemed to make more sense. Although he said some things about Jesus Christ that seemed strange to me, I was interested in how he connected the New Testament with the Old. Starting in the book of Matthew, Oleg tried to explain the fulfillment of the Old Testament prophecies in the life of Jesus.

While I was listening on the outside, I was laughing on the inside. *He expects me to believe this? Just because he says a prophecy was fulfilled in Jesus Christ, I'm supposed to believe it was really fulfilled? Oleg and Matthew might be saying this, but that doesn't mean that I'm convinced.* I had just finished reading the book of Matthew for myself, and it hadn't impressed me at all.

But while Oleg's arguments didn't sway me, his personality did. At the end of the meeting he came over to me and said, "Welcome back. Nicholai told me about you. I hear that you are studying in a rabbinical school. I've never met anyone who was studying to become a rabbi.

"You know, you Jews really have some advantages over us in understanding the Old Testament. If you have something you could give me to read I would appreciate it very much."

What a neat guy! I thought. *I will definitely be glad to give him something to read so that he can understand what real Jews write. I don't want him to think that the Gospels are the only Jewish writings after the Tanakh!* Quickly running up to my room, I grabbed *The Teachings of the Fathers. This will be nice for him to read,* I thought. *He will become acquainted with some of our wise teachers.* Running back down to Room 421, I handed the book to Oleg. "I'll start reading it tonight," he said.

CHAPTER 16

ALL ISRAEL

HAVE A PORTION

IN THE WORLD TO COME,

FOR IT IS WRITTEN,

"THY PEOPLE ARE ALL

RIGHTEOUS;

THEY SHALL INHERIT

THE LAND FOR EVER,

THE BRANCH

OF MY PLANTING,

THE WORK OF MY HANDS,

THAT I MAY BE

GLORIFIED."

BUT THE FOLLOWING

HAVE NO PORTION

THEREIN: HE WHO

MAINTAINS THAT

RESURRECTION IS NOT

A BIBLICAL DOCTRINE . . . .

—*Talmud, Sanhedrin 90a*

One week later I visited Oleg in his room. "What an interesting book!" he said excitedly. "It contains so much wisdom, and one can gain so many spiritual lessons from reading it." I was happy that Oleg had liked the book.

Then he said, "I have a question for you, since you've no doubt read a lot of Jewish literature. Tell me how you understand the specific prophecies that predict the coming of the Messiah."

"Well," I replied, "what's the problem? I know that Messiah is coming very soon. Our great rabbis have told us how wonderful it will be when Messiah arrives. All Jews will gather in Jerusalem, and they will become a great nation.

"I must give you a book by our great rabbi Maimonides. He predicted many centuries ago a restoration of the state of Israel, followed by a great war. Messiah will help us win this war and rebuild the Temple. His prophecy, given in the twelfth century, is being fulfilled."

Oleg was listening carefully, so I continued. "You see, there is now a state of Israel, and it looks as if a war could break out in the near future, so I am sure that there is not much time left until we will see our Messiah."

After thinking for a few moments, Oleg responded, "What do you think about where Messiah should be born?"

As I considered his question, I realized it brought me to a dead end. I didn't have an answer. I really didn't know where Messiah was supposed to be born.

Oleg opened his Bible and showed me Micah 5:2-5: "'But as for you, Bethlehem Ephrathah, too little to be among the clans of Judah, from you One will go forth for Me to be ruler in Israel. His goings forth are from long ago, from the days of eternity.' . . . And He will arise and shepherd His flock in the strength of the Lord, in the majesty of the name of the Lord His God. And they will remain, because at that time He will be great to the ends of the earth. And this One will be our peace" (NASB). It was clear to me that the passage definitely spoke about the Messiah.

"You've probably read the Gospel of Matthew," Oleg said. "Jesus was born in Bethlehem, as this prophecy predicts."

"What's the big deal?" I replied. "How many people have been born in Bethlehem during the past 2,000 years? Which one is the Messiah? I don't question that Jesus was born in Bethlehem—it's clear that he was. But that still doesn't give him the right to be the Messiah just because he was born in Bethlehem. And you don't need to point out to me that Matthew shows that sometime after his birth in Bethlehem Jesus moved to Nazareth—I've already read that. But still, how many people were born in Bethlehem, and then moved to Nazareth? Which of them is the Messiah? And maybe Messiah has not even been born yet."

Oleg scratched his head. It seemed that he didn't know what to say, so I continued. "I should give you another book. Have you ever heard of the *Mishneh Torah*? It is the great work of our teacher Rambam. You read it and see what he believes about the Messiah." Oleg took the book and left.

Three days later Oleg knocked at my door. Entering, he said, "This book has some very interesting points. And it corresponds with the New Testament."

This is crazy! I thought. *Rambam is the one who said in his book* Moreh Nevukhim *("Guide for the Perplexed") that the one who even touches the New Testament is a traitor! How could it be that any of his thoughts would correspond to the New Testament?*

"In New Testament times," Oleg went on, "many Jews believed that the Messiah was going to be a great warrior who would free all Jews from the Roman yoke. Your rabbi, Rambam, was thinking this same way. But I can see that he was a very wise person. I would be most interested to see what he thinks of the passage found in Isaiah 53."

What's in Isaiah 53? I wondered. I had never read Isaiah 53, nor had I ever heard that part of the book of Isaiah read at the yeshiva or at any services at the synagogue. After Oleg left I turned to Isaiah 53:

"He is despised and rejected by men, a Man of sorrows and acquainted with grief. And we hid, as it were, our faces from Him; He was despised, and we did not esteem Him" (verse 3, NKJV). *Whom is Isaiah talking about?* I wondered. *And why does Oleg think that this is a picture of the Messiah?*

I continued reading. "Surely He has borne our griefs and carried our sorrows; yet we esteemed Him stricken, smitten by God, and afflicted. But He was wounded for our transgressions, He was bruised for our iniquities; the chastisement for our peace was upon Him, and by His stripes we are healed. . . . He was oppressed and He was afflicted, yet He opened not His mouth; He was led as a lamb to the slaughter, and as a sheep before its shearers is silent, so He opened not His mouth" (verses 4-6, NKJV).

I had never read about this suffering servant before, and after going through the entire chapter of Isaiah 53, I felt troubled and confused. How could the passage be depicting the Messiah—the One who will bring happiness and joy and will make Israel a great nation? And why would Messiah have to suffer if He is coming to deliver us?

After thinking about these questions for a couple weeks, I finally approached Oleg about the passage. "What's the problem?" he asked. "What you are saying is true, but you are thinking about His second coming. He does plan to return to this earth again to save all humanity and to build up His kingdom, and we are expecting His coming. Christianity is not a religion based upon a dead person. Our Messiah is alive, but when He was here on earth He *did* take our infirmities and carry our sorrows. He *was* pierced for our transgressions and cursed for our iniquities. The punishment of the world *was* upon Him, and 'with His stripes we are healed.' He died for our sins, but we are expecting Him again—and this time He will arrive in glory and majesty and make our earth new."

"Well," I said happily, "we have something in common. We are expecting the Messiah, and so are you. It looks like our expectations are similar. I think our problem can be solved easily, because I believe He is coming very soon. When He arrives, we can just ask Him if He has already come the first time or not!"

"That is a very interesting suggestion," Oleg replied. "The only question is How do you know that you will be saved? You probably believe the same as we do about the Messiah being very righteous, and if you have sins and don't put them upon His shoulders now, then when He comes He is not going to save you from sin, but will redeem only His already saved ones. How are you going to atone for all the sins you are committing now?"

"That's no problem," I said. "We have the writings of our rabbis and we have the Torah, which contains 613 commandments. We just keep them, and that makes us right before God."

I thought Oleg's eyes were going to pop out of his head. "Six hundred thirteen?" he exclaimed. "That's a lot! How do you know if you're keeping them all? And what if you break one? Then what are you going to do?"

This guy is a real problem, I thought to myself. "Haven't you read the *Mishneh Torah* I gave you?" I asked him. "Rambam says that since we no longer have a Temple with its services, the only way to be forgiven of our sins is through our sincere repentance."

"Yes, I read that," Oleg said. "But how could he so easily pass over his own Torah? The Torah strictly requires a sacrifice for *every* sin, big or small. Doesn't he believe in the Torah?" I didn't know what to say. Naturally I couldn't believe that the great Rambam didn't believe in the Torah! There had to be an answer somewhere to all of these difficult questions, and I decided to search for it.

It was late Friday night when I left Oleg's room. As I was walking along the long corridor to my room, I thought to myself, *Am I really keeping all 613 commandments?*

I already knew that I was planning to break a commandment the very next day—the Sabbath. I believed in the Sabbath, but to be honest, I knew I wasn't really keeping it holy. Often we would have Friday afternoon *Minchah* (prayer) at the synagogue, followed at sunset with the *Maariv* service. But frequently we would not have any Sabbath services at the synagogue, because of the shortage of rabbis. So when there were important events at the university on Sabbath, such as exams, I would participate in them.

After talking with Oleg, I found myself faced with a dilemma. I was scheduled to take an exam on differential equations the next morning. I enjoyed the class immensely and had been faithfully preparing for the exam for weeks. For the first time the question arose in my mind—should I take it on Sabbath? What should I do? Should I deliberately break a commandment and then sincerely repent? Somehow that seemed hypocritical.

That night as I wrestled with my plans for the following day, I made a decision. *If God is real,* I thought, *if He really wants me to keep His commandments, then He must do something to show me that this is what He desires.* At last I was able to fall asleep for a few hours.

The next morning I went to the exam. After spending about 45 minutes answering all of the written questions, I went up to the professor to receive my oral question. As my professor looked over my written work, I saw his face growing more and more somber. I couldn't understand what the problem was, because I knew the teacher well, and he knew that differential equations was one of my best subjects.

Finally he said, "Bolotnikov, I'm sorry, but you haven't solved *any* of the problems correctly. Something must be going on with you today, or you're sick or something. Go home and come back in five days when you're feeling better, and you can retake the exam."

That was my answer. God was real! He had heard what I said to Him in my prayer, and He had given me a direct response. *No,* I thought to myself. *I shouldn't do this thing ever again. If He's so real, He will be helping me with my next classes and the exams on Sabbath.* I never went to class or attempted to take an exam on Sabbath again.

CHAPTER 17

Life in the dormitory was becoming difficult. My roommate, Chaika, was drinking more and more, often bringing others to our room, where they would spend most of the night consuming vodka and listening to loud rock music.

"Judas," he sputtered out one day, "what are you doing, still going to those Christian meetings down the hall? Have you forgotten that you're a Jew?" He started to laugh, but I didn't think it was so funny.

More than three months had passed since Chaika's suggestion that we visit the "cannibals' room," and during that time I had experienced warmth and friendship from them—even if they were Christians! During the year and a half that I had been studying at the synagogue I hadn't been able to form any real, close friendships, as people were coming and going to Israel and there were no permanent students.

The Christian study group didn't meet in Room 421 anymore, since it had received permission to use a small room located between two wings of the dormitory. The room was open every evening for prayer and fellowship, and I knew that I could go there and always find someone to talk to. It helped me a lot with my feelings of loneliness.

The group also had regular Bible studies each week. The Pentecostals had organized it, although a couple Baptists and one or two other Christians had joined the group as well.

During the course of a year the Pentecostals invited their pastor to speak to our group 10 times. The man didn't make much of an impression on me. While it was apparent that he was a sincere believer, it seemed that he didn't have much intelligence. His clothing was in constant disrepair, and so was his manner of speech. He made his living by working as a night security guard at a nearby airport.

His presentations usually focused on three topics: (1) prayer; (2) sins and how to cleanse yourself from sin; and (3) spiritual gifts. He never preached from the Bible. Instead he addressed the topics using his own life experiences and by giving advice. Every now and then he would bring a "prophet" with him to our group.

The first time I saw the prophet, I could see that he was a very proud man. His primary prophetic focus was on reproving the secret sins of young people. He shared with us some of his rebukes to young men who lustfully gazed at girls or who were doing something even worse.

The man told us about one of his prophecies that had already come true. He had predicted judgment upon one especially bad sinner. A short time later the poor individual died in a car accident. The prophet was extremely proud of this, and thus based his "gift of prophecy" upon the fulfillment of his predictions. I didn't like his meetings, and usually left the room before they ended.

Oleg and Nicholai could sense that I wasn't impressed with their pastor or their prophet.

"Don't pay attention to the outward appearance, Sasha, or even the manner of speech. Man looks upon the outward appearance, but God looks upon the heart." Although they quoted to me from the Tanakh to support their statements, I still wasn't convinced.

One day Oleg asked, "Sasha, why don't you come with me to our church this Sunday?" Briefly mulling the invitation over, I remembered the terrifying experience Nadia and I went through at the Orthodox church. But Oleg and Nicholai weren't anti-Semitic, so I reasoned that their church must not be either.

"OK," I said. "I'll go."

At 8:30 Sunday morning Oleg was at my door, ready to attend church. I didn't figure that I'd need a head covering, but I tucked a handkerchief into my pocket just in case.

Walking out of the dormitory, we headed toward Kharkov Road, where we caught a tram headed east. The Pentecostal church was located in a big apartment building where the pastor lived. Since he had seven children, the government had given him two adjoining two-bedroom apartments on the same floor. The members had knocked the wall out between the two apartments, creating a large room that they used for their worship services.

As Oleg and I entered the room, the service was about to start. I noticed that the room was divided into two distinct halves—a women's side and a men's side. Taking a seat on the men's side, I looked over to the other side of the room. Even though I knew that there must be women over there, it was hard to tell, because they were all wearing large, heavy scarves draped over their heads, covering the sides of their cheeks and necks. Their skirts came down nearly to their ankles, and I noticed that they all wore thick dark stockings, even though it wasn't cold outside.

When I asked Oleg about this, he explained that Christ said in the book of Matthew that if a man has even looked at a woman in lust he has already committed adultery with her in his heart.

"But how do you ever find someone to marry?" I asked. Oleg

explained that if a young man likes a certain unmarried girl in the congregation, and if a strange sensation comes into his heart when he looks at her, then he must quickly go to the pastor and tell him which girl causes the special feelings. The pastor then visits the girl's home and speaks with the parents and the girl. He says something like "Listen, Brother Ivan is a very good man and has never fallen into sin. He has been faithful to the Lord, but when he sees your daughter something happens in his mind and heart, and you know what Christ has said about that. So, sister, I think that you are a good Christian and you won't let this brother fall into sin." Then if the girl agrees, they arrange a marriage.

What a strange religion, I thought.

After the pastor gave his sermon, five men from the congregation stood up and shared their thoughts along the same lines as the sermon. Altogether this took about 45 minutes. Then the prayer time began. I remained sitting in my chair while everyone else in the room went down on their knees.

Suddenly a loud babbling began in the front of the room, and I wondered if someone had gotten sick. Quickly the epidemic spread around the room as people all around me started making strange noises, accompanied by intermittent groaning. Some swayed back and forth; others were on their hands and knees. *This has got to be the craziest place on earth!* I decided, observing what was going on all around me.

Wondering how long the phenomenon would last, I kept glancing from the people to the watch on my wrist. The noise seemed to grow louder and louder, finally reaching a peak and gradually calming down. The "prayer" process took more than an hour. Finally I could escape.

Once we were out on the street, Oleg asked me how I liked the meeting. "It was fine," I mumbled. But in my own mind I decided that I would never, ever step inside such a crazy place again.

CHAPTER 18

PEACE

I LEAVE WITH YOU,

MY PEACE

I GIVE UNTO YOU:

NOT AS THE WORLD

GIVETH,

GIVE I UNTO YOU.

LET NOT

YOUR HEART

BE TROUBLED,

NEITHER

LET IT BE AFRAID.

—John 14:27

Although I was not impressed by my experience at Oleg's church, I continued meeting with the small group of Christians in the dormitory. During the five months I had associated with them, I had been thinking more and more about God and was experiencing a closeness with Him that I had never felt before. The discussions we had about the Christian life—modesty, purity, and piety— made me think more about how I was living my own life according to the law of Moses, which I really never kept very well. These Christians were helping me to understand my Creator as a person, not just as the object of my national pride or as a subject for theological discussions.

Nevertheless, even though I associated with the Christian group, I still continued going regularly to the synagogue. One of the reasons I kept attending was to find an answer to the question Oleg had raised with me about the "suffering servant" described in Isaiah 53. *Who was this suffering servant?* I continued asking myself. Surely the answer had to be somewhere.

I was afraid to ask the rabbi, because he might wonder where I came up with such a question. If he knew I was associating with Christians—especially if he discovered that I was actually attending their small Bible study group—he would certainly condemn me. I remembered his violent reaction to the New Testaments someone had placed in our hands at Babi Yar, and I did not want to be a recipient of his curse! So rather than asking about Isaiah 53, I spent many long evenings in the yeshiva library browsing through various books and commentaries, trying to find the answer about the strange servant slain for the sins of the whole world.

One day, after several months of research, I found the answer I was looking for. It was located in an interesting commentary by one of the greatest rabbis of the Middle Ages—Rashi, Rabbi Solomon, son of Isaac. In referring to Isaiah 53, Rashi quoted Isaiah 44:21—"Remember these, O Jacob, and Israel, for you are my servant; I have formed you, you are my servant; O Israel, you will not be forgotten by Me!" (NKJV).

According to Rashi, Isaiah identified the "suffering servant" of Isaiah 53 as Jacob—Israel! *Of course!* I thought. *This servant that has been suffering like a lamb is God's people—Israel!* Israel had endured persecution for more than 1,500 years since the destruction of Jerusalem. That was well documented.

The little horn of Daniel 7:25 came to my mind—"He . . . shall persecute the saints of the Most High" (NKJV). The saints of the Most High—the Jewish people, of course! It all seemed to be fitting together again. The little horn, Christ, is speaking pompous words against God and changing the law and the holy days. He persecutes the saints, the holy nation of Israel, whom God identifies in Isaiah 53 as His suffering servant. I was pleased that at last I had an answer for Oleg.

When I shared it with him a few days later, he didn't seem convinced that the suffering servant was the nation of Israel. "How could their lives make atonement for the sins of the whole world?" he asked. It was another good question for which I did not have a good answer.

I wondered how it was that Oleg, a Christian, had such a strong knowledge of the Tanakh. The Orthodox Christians I knew did not pay much attention to it. In fact, the Russian translation of the Bible even called it the *Vetkheey,* that is, "Dilapidated" Testament. Orthodox believers claimed the "New Testament" as the main guide for Christians, saying that the Dilapidated Testament was just a historical narrative of how some people fell into sin and what happened to them and so on, but that Jesus had changed everything and had given completely new commandments, so they wouldn't pay too much attention to the Dilapidated Testament. So why then did Oleg and my other Protestant friends seem so interested in, and knowledgeable about, the Old Testament?

By this time I had completely forgotten that my original purpose for joining the little group of Christians was to show them that Christ was the little horn in Daniel 7. They were nice and different from the other inhabitants of our dormitory. The study group members didn't need a bottle of vodka and a pack of cigarettes in order to speak about deep things. Sensitive to my feelings, they always made me feel welcome at their meetings.

However, I still couldn't make a connection between the Orthodox Christian view of the Tanakh as the Dilapidated Testament and their interest in this book. So one day while we were meeting together, I decided to ask Oleg a question in front of the whole group. "Tell me," I said, "do you really believe that the Old Testament is the inspired Word of God?"

Nicholai, who was sitting right beside me, responded first. "Definitely, yes! We believe that the Old Testament is an inspired holy book and is part of the Holy Bible."

Then Oleg added, "If I didn't believe in the Old Testament as a holy book, how could I ever believe that Christ came to this world, lived, died, and rose again according to the prophets? Which prophets is the New Testament talking about? Of course, the prophets from the Old Testament."

Their response intrigued me, but I couldn't hold back another question that had found its way to the tip of my tongue.

"If you believe that the Old Testament is the inspired Word of God, don't you know that it speaks of Sabbath as the holy day? So why do you keep Sunday?"

The room remained silent for about three minutes. Oleg looked at Nicholai; Nicholai glanced at Oleg. The eight other students in the group stared at each other, searching for an answer to my pointed question. During this long silence I noticed a new guy sitting toward the back of the small room. He wasn't looking at anyone. Then slowly he stood up and said, "I cannot speak for the rest of the group, but I am a Seventh-day Adventist, and I keep the Sabbath day holy. I am a Christian. I believe that Christ has died for my sins and through His blood I receive redemption. But I still believe that we need to adhere to the whole Bible, including the Ten Commandments of God's holy law and the laws of clean and unclean food."

His statement shocked me. *What kind of Christian is this,* I wondered, *that keeps the Sabbath day holy and even adheres to the laws of kashrut (the laws that determine clean and unclean foods)?* Immediately I felt a special bond with this Christian and started calling him "colleague."

The more time I spent with Tolik, my new Christian friend, the more I grew to love and respect him. I kept thinking about what a smart man he must be to have discovered in his Bible that God's holy day is really Sabbath in spite of the traditional Christian view of Sunday as being the day of worship. And he had even accepted the laws of *kashrut!*

The only problem I felt that Tolik seemed to have was his belief in this liar—Jesus—as his God and Saviour. However, I was sympathetic toward him. He was born into a Christian Russian family, so it wasn't unusual for him to think of Christ as God.

But I determined that this soul should not be lost. He should be brought to Judaism. So Tolik became my major object of attention.

Not long after I became acquainted with Tolik, our study group had an interesting discussion about the "gift of tongues." Since I had never read about this "gift" in the Tanakh, I listened quietly as the Pentecostals and Baptists argued back and forth. Finally Tolik, the only Seventh-day Adventist in the group, suggested that the best person to answer the question would be his pastor, since he was neither Pentecostal nor Baptist.

The following week Pastor Yuri Grigoriyevich Kuzmenko came to our Bible study group. He immediately impressed me. Here was a man who dressed neatly and respectably. Although he worked as a plumber and had not received any special theological training, it was not difficult to see that he had a deep knowledge of the Scriptures. Speaking clearly and logically, he turned methodically from passage to passage in the New Testament that mentioned the gift of tongues. It was obvious that he knew the writings of Paul well. It impressed the Pentecostals as well as me.

Rather than going to the synagogue alone the next Friday evening, I went to church with Tolik instead. The church was located in a large house converted into a place of worship. A large room served as the sanctuary. It even had a balcony, which impressed me because it reminded me of the synagogue. However, unlike the synagogue, women were welcome to sit on the main floor if they wished.

Something else that really impressed me was a large picture of two tables of stone with the Ten Commandments on them hanging prominently at the front of the sanctuary, right behind the pulpit.

The pastor's sermon was again clear and logical, just as his presentation had been to our small study group in the dormitory. Using both the Old and New Testaments, he showed the importance of keeping the Sabbath day holy. The only part of the sermon I didn't like was when the pastor said that we needed to pray to Christ to help those who were having problems with work on Sabbath. But other than the one reference to Christ, I felt very much at home during the worship service.

Heading back to the dormitory that Friday night, I was excited. How neat it was to see 500 people who believed in the Ten Commandments, who kept the Sabbath day holy, and who ate only "clean foods." These people were ready to be circumcised! I wanted them to know about and experience the great inheritance that the people of the Jewish faith possessed. The only problem was that they believed that Jesus Christ was the Son of God. I decided that there must be something I could do to lead these special people to Judaism.

CHAPTER 19

One evening not long after my visit to the Seventh-day Adventist church, I went to see Tolik in his dorm room. As I entered, I overheard him quickly whispering to a friend, "This man is Jewish, studying at the synagogue. Very interested, but please don't use the name of Christ in his presence." It impressed me that Tolik was sensitive and careful to respect my feelings.

I soon learned that Tolik's friend, Sergei, was also a Seventh-day Adventist. He asked me questions about the synagogue and Jewish traditions. I happened to have my *Taniya* ("Collection of Speeches"), by Rabbi Schneur Zalman, with me. It was the book I had purchased after my first visit to the synagogue in Kiev. Fascinated with the Hebrew characters, Sergei kept looking at the book and asking me questions about its contents. I was glad to share with him some of the profound philosophical truths about the Godhead I had discovered from reading the book. Sergei listened patiently. I was happy he was so interested.

After Sergei left, I turned to Tolik and asked, "May I ask you a sincere question?"

"Of course," he answered.

"Are you really sure that Christ, whom you worship on Sabbath, is a real God whom you should worship?"

"Well," Tolik said, "I believe He is. At least the Bible prophecies of the Old Testament predict His coming."

Opening his Bible, he continued, "What would you say, for example, about Micah 5:2: 'But as for you, Bethlehem Ephrathah, too little to be among the clans of Judah, from you One will go forth for Me to be ruler in Israel. His goings forth are from long ago, from the days of eternity' [NASB]?"

Well, I thought, remembering my discussion with Oleg several weeks earlier, *I've heard all of these Christian arguments before. This will be no big deal.*

"Yes," I told Tolik, "I believe that this text proves that the Messiah will be born in Bethlehem, but how in the world can you prove that it refers specifically to Jesus Christ? How many babies have been born in Bethlehem and how many are still being born there? Maybe one day one of them will be the Messiah, but not yet."

"You have a good point," Tolik replied. "But the Old Testament has many other prophecies about Jesus. For example, there's Isaiah 53:3-5: 'He is despised and rejected of men; a man of sorrows, and acquainted with grief: and we hid as it were our faces from him; he was despised, and we esteemed him not. Surely he hath borne our griefs, and carried our sorrows: yet we did esteem him stricken, smitten of God, and afflicted. But he was wounded for our transgressions, he was bruised for our iniquities: the chastisement of our peace was upon him; and with his stripes we are healed.'

"I've always wondered about the Jewish viewpoint on these

Old Testament passages," he added. This also was going to be easy, I thought, because I had already covered the "suffering servant" issue with Oleg and Nicholai. I was ready with my answer and shared with him my discovery in Isaiah 44 that the suffering servant was Jacob/Israel.

"This is the same Isaiah writing, isn't it? But here he is writing that God's servant is Jacob/Israel, not the Messiah. So Isaiah 53 must refer to Jacob/Israel, that is, the Jewish people, who have suffered from the persecution Christians have committed against them. We were really bruised and pierced during the Middle Ages and the pogroms."

Since Tolik was listening intently, I became even bolder. "By the way, let me show you that the Bible even predicted these persecutions, and you will find out something very interesting about your Jesus Christ."

Taking Tolik's Bible, I turned to Daniel 7:25: "And he shall speak great words against the most High, and shall wear out the saints of the most High, and think to change times and laws."

"Who is this little horn?" I asked. "Who fights with the saints of the Most High and who changes the holy day and the law, which you believe should be obeyed? Look at the Christian church. Who among the Christians believe in the seventh-day Sabbath except for you Adventists?

"You know your math pretty well, Tolik. If 'a' equals 'b' and 'c' equals 'b,' it means that 'c' and 'a' are the same thing. So if Christ originated the Christian church, with all of its false worship on Sunday, and the little horn tries to change the Sabbath into Sunday, who do you think Christ is? Isn't he the little horn in Daniel 7?"

Tolik was still listening, so I continued. "I think you Adventists are good people, but your theology has a big inconsistency. You cannot believe in the seventh-day Sabbath and at the same time believe in Jesus Christ, who originated the change from Sabbath to Sunday!"

Watching Tolik closely, I wondered why he was so quiet. I couldn't understand why he wasn't objecting to my arguments, especially when I mentioned the Christian church. Finally he spoke. And what he had to say was even more shocking than his silence.

"Sasha," he said, "Seventh-day Adventists agree with almost everything you have just said."

I couldn't believe what I was hearing.

"We believe," he went on, "that the Christian church has apostatized from the principles of the Bible. We believe that the change from Sabbath to Sunday is a direct act of the church, not supported by the Bible.[1]

"Where I cannot agree with you is in your identification of Jesus Christ as the little horn in Daniel 7. It is true that Christians have hated the Jews throughout the centuries. And it is also true that the state churches have persecuted Jews in Russia and Europe, but you cannot blame Christ for originating this. Christ loves every person."

Taking his Bible, Tolik opened it to the book of John and started reading: "'God so loved the world that He gave His only begotten Son, that *whoever* believes in Him should not perish but have everlasting life'" (John 3:16, NKJV).

"See what it says?" Tolik pointed at the verse. "Christ doesn't want *anyone* to perish. Not even the Jews. You know, He Himself was Jewish, and He loves everyone. How can He not love His own people?"

"Well," I objected, "I know some Conservative Jewish rabbis[2] who believe that Christ was a good teacher, but the apostles were the ones who tried to make him into a God and changed all Jewish rituals."

"I disagree with you," Tolik said. "Did you know that the apostles kept the Sabbath holy? Look at Acts 13:14: 'But when they departed from Perga, they came to Antioch in Pisidia, and went into the synagogue on the Sabbath day and sat down' [NKJV]. And look at verses 42 and 44," Tolik continued. "'So when the Jews went out of the synagogue, the Gentiles begged that these words might be preached to them the next Sabbath. . . . On the next Sabbath almost the whole city came together to hear the word of God' [NKJV].

"The apostles went to the synagogue on Sabbath," Tolik repeated. "They didn't go only to the Jews, but they also called the Gentiles to the synagogue on Sabbath. Paul never tried to change the day of worship from Sabbath to Sunday."

His evidence hit me really hard. It reminded me of my shocking discovery in Hebrews 4:9 when I learned that the Christian New Testament did not forbid worship on Sabbath. But now, to see where Paul was actually preaching to *Gentiles* on the Sabbath . . . this was something I had never expected. I felt as if all my arguments, which I had based on Daniel 7, were melting away.

"I think," Tolik said, as if he could read my thoughts, "that your problem with the little horn in Daniel 7 will be solved when you read a little bit further down through chapter 9. I would like to suggest that you go back to your room, get your Old Testament, and read."

As I wandered down the long corridor back to my own room, I wondered what I would find in Daniel 9. And how was it that Tolik agreed with almost everything I said? Why did he seem to have a better understanding of the Tanakh than I, a Jew, did?

Approaching the door of my room, I was relieved to hear silence rather than the usual driving beat and high-pitched screeching that my roommate enjoyed listening to on his tape player.

Finding myself alone in the room, I decided to take a look at Daniel 9. I began scanning the chapter, looking for a key to unlock my many questions. As I searched the chapter, verses 24-26 seemed to stand out:

"Seventy weeks are determined for your people and for your holy city, to finish the transgression, to make an end of sins, to make reconciliation for iniquity, to bring in everlasting righteousness, to seal up vision and prophecy, and to anoint the Most Holy.

"Know therefore and understand, that from the going forth of the command to restore and build Jerusalem until Messiah the Prince, there shall be seven weeks and sixty-two weeks; the street shall be built again, and the wall, even in troublesome times.

"And after the sixty-two weeks Messiah shall be cut off, but not for Himself; and the people of the prince who is to come shall destroy the city and the sanctuary. The end of it shall be with a flood, and till the end of the war desolations are determined" (NKJV).

Seventy weeks, I thought. *Very interesting point. Seventy weeks equals 490 days.* I vividly remembered a lecture at the yeshiva when a visiting rabbi from Israel had told us that the Israelites had to wander the desert for 40 years because they had rebelled for 40 days when they were at the border of Canaan—so it was one year for each day of rebellion.

I was also aware of the passage in Ezekiel 4:6: "I have laid on you a day for each year" (NKJV). This year-for-a-day principle appeared elsewhere in the Sacred Writings, so I had no doubt that Daniel was talking about years rather than literal days in his prophecy.

As I continued to look at the passage, I was especially troubled by the part that said the *Mashiah*[3] would be "cut off." Here was a new concept. I had never thought that Mashiah would have to die. How could this be? I knew that the great rabbi Rambam wrote about the coming of the Mashiah and the restoration of the Temple. But why should Mashiah die?

But the scariest part of the whole Daniel 9 passage was the second part of verse 26: "And the people of the prince who is to come shall destroy the city and the sanctuary" (NKJV).

What is this talking about? Is there going to be another *de-*

struction after the Temple's restoration, or could it be that this was something that has already happened in the past? Quickly I realized that the one way to discover the answer was to calculate the 70-week time period. And just from a cursory reading of the passage it wasn't difficult to guesstimate approximately where the 70 weeks would lead.

Suddenly a terrible thought came ripping through my mind: "Blasted by the bones of the ones who calculate the time of the end!"[4] The rabbi at the yeshiva had quoted this powerful curse from the Talmud on the day he burned the New Testaments given to us at Babi Yar. During his fiery lecture to us that day he had listed some of the Old Testament passages that Christians use to try to convert Jews. Daniel 9 had been one of them.

"It is strictly prohibited to calculate these 70 weeks," the rabbi declared. "This terrible curse will fall upon anyone who tries to calculate this 70-week time period."

I knew that the curse of "blasted bones" was the worst possible curse anyone could receive. It was the same kind of curse described in the first two verses of Ezekiel 37, in which the prophet sees a valley strewn with dry bones. The bones were cursed bones—that's why they were "blasted" all over the dry valley floor.

Deciding that I didn't want my future to consist of blasted bones, I closed my Old Testament and tried to forget about calculating the time.

But the thought refused to go away. What could be lurking in this forbidden chapter?

One night, as I was taking the train home to Kuznetsovsk, I couldn't sleep. The persistent question kept circling my mind— Should I calculate it? Should I calculate it? I was afraid to do it, because I already realized that the dates would bring me close to the time of Christ.

Tossing back and forth, I at last fell into a restless twilight sleep. All of a sudden it seemed that someone was reading to me from the book of Matthew: "Behold, the hour is at hand, and the Son of Man is being betrayed into the hands of sinners" (Matt. 26:4, 5, NKJV).

The voice repeated the text again and again, and I felt a heavy weight pressing down on me. "The Son of Man, the Son of Man, the Son of Man . . ." the phrase repeated in rhythm with the train wheels on the railroad tracks.

I woke up with a start. What was the meaning of this strange experience? Again I was impressed that I needed to calculate the 70-week time period, but I was afraid. I knew that the only bit of information I needed to calculate this time was the date when the decree went out to restore the Temple in Jerusalem.

A few weeks after returning to Kiev from my visit home, I was back in the yeshiva library. The question in my mind about the 70 weeks still begged for an answer. As I was casually browsing through some books on the table, I nonchalantly turned to Chaim and asked, "In which year do you think Ezra received permission to rebuild Jerusalem?"

"Oh, about 460 or 450 B.C.E.," he responded.

This is it, I thought to myself. Quickly adding 483 prophetic "days" (or 69 "weeks"), I arrived at 30 or 35 C.E. I knew immediately that it stretched to the time of Jesus Christ. Everyone knew that. But this discovery meant that Daniel had predicted the destruction of the Temple and that he pointed to Jesus as the Mashiah. Impossible! I could never accept that!

---

[1] See Holtsman, *The Canon and Tradition,* p. 263, cited in Mark Finley, *The Great Prophecies of the Bible.*

[2] A Conservative Jew is more liberal than an Orthodox or Hasidic Jew.

[3] *Mashiah* is "Messiah" in Hebrew.

[4] Talmud, Sanhedrin 97b, the footnote commentary to this saying of Rabbi Samuel b. Nahmani states that the rabbi meant the time of the Messiah advent.

CHAPTER 20

I tried to forget my discovery in Daniel 9, but my mind was still churning. If my calculations were right, and this prophecy did indeed predict Jesus as the Mashiah and the destruction of the Temple, then why hadn't our great rabbis discovered this? What about Maimonides? Rashi? Or our great Rabbi Schneur Zalman? Why hadn't they come to the same conclusions?

And why in the world did the Talmud curse anyone who attempted to calculate the 70-week time period of Daniel 9? It seemed that the rabbis who wrote the Talmud were smart enough to have calculated the time, otherwise why would they have written the curse? They knew the writings well enough to have discovered this strange prophecy.

One day during this dark time, when I seemed to have many important questions and no answers, I noticed an interesting little tract for sale at the synagogue. Titled *Yud Beit Tamuz* ("The Eleventh of Tammuz"—

the month corresponding to June and July), the tract was about the great Rabbi Yosef Yitzchak Schneerson. I decided to buy it and began reading it on the way back to my university dormitory.

As I read, I became more and more interested in Rabbi Schneerson. He had been sentenced to death by Stalin, but was suddenly released from prison under rather strange circumstances and allowed to emigrate to the United States in 1928. The tract claimed that the United States government had set the possibility of establishing diplomatic relations with the U.S.S.R. upon condition that it would release Schneerson from prison. Not only did it allow Schneerson to leave, but many other Jews of the Lubavicher Hasidic movement[1] received permission to follow Schneerson to America.

· This miraculous event greatly impressed the followers of Lubavicher Hasidism as well as Schneerson himself. He decided to dedicate the last years of his life to preaching the soon-coming Mashiah. Soon after his arrival in the U.S., Schneerson proclaimed: "It remains [for] us to polish the buttons of our uniforms so that we will be ready to go out and greet our Righteous Mashiah."[2]

Later, in 1941, when Hitler attacked Russia, Schneerson proclaimed from his home in the U.S.: "Mashiah is already here: 'Here he stands behind our wall' (Song of Songs 2:9). In a higher world there is rejoicing already: he has already come: down here, however, he is waiting for the Jewish people to repent."[3]

Shortly before his death in 1949, Schneerson again said: "What are people waiting for? The redemption is being held up!"[4]

I liked the idea of a soon-coming Mashiah. And if this good rabbi believed Mashiah could come in the 1930s or 1940s, how much closer His coming must be now in 1990!

The more I thought about this, the more excited I became. If the Mashiah's arrival was imminent, then I could ask Him all of my questions, including the mysteries of Daniel 7 and 9. Mashiah would know the truth and would be able to unravel all of these perplexing problems that weighed so heavily upon my mind.

A few weeks later my excitement grew to fever pitch when, in June 1990, a guest rabbi from New York visited our yeshiva. He had a very long beard, but was dressed in an ordinary suit rather than the *lopserdockst* that we were used to our rabbis wearing. However, we could see the traditional Orthodox *tsitsit* fringes hanging below his suit jacket.

Standing, the visiting rabbi greeted us and said, "I have something to tell you from our great Rabbi Schneerson." Since I knew that the Rabbi Yosef Yitzchak Schneerson had died in 1949, I realized that the message must be from his son-in-law and successor—Rabbi Menachem Mendel Schneerson.

The visiting rabbi pulled out a letter from Rabbi Schneerson and read: "What more can I do to motivate the entire Jewish race to clamor and cry out, and thus bring about the coming of Mashiah? . . .

"Now, do everything you can to bring Mashiah, here and now, immediately."[5]

The rabbi looked up and asked us, "Why is Rabbi Schneerson saying these things?" We were silent, since we didn't know. The visiting rabbi then explained to us what had been taking place within Hasidic Judaism in the United States during the past year.

Rabbi Schneerson had been carefully studying the *Taniya,* written by Rabbi Schneur Zalman at the end of the eighteenth century. According to Zalman, the Mashiah was to come and the believing Jewish people were to be redeemed by the beginning of the second half of the sixth millennium[6] (the beginning of the eighteenth century), but at that time they were not found worthy. However, since He did not come at that time, He would definitely arrive before the end of the current millennium.[7] Because the Mashiah's coming was imminent, Rabbi Schneerson had been giving special attention to this subject. "On June 3, 1989, Rabbi Schneerson noticed that the numerical value of the coming year

חש יינ formed an acronym of Hebrew words: תהא שנת נסים—'this will be a year of miracles.' "

Excitement mounted throughout the room, as the rabbi him-self became more animated. "And *this* year, in fact just *last month* on May 12 [1990], Rabbi Schneerson found that the numerical equivalent of the Hebrew letters for the coming year, תשנ"א, are as-sociated with the Hebrew words תהא שנת אדאנו נפלאות—'This will be a year when I [God] will show you wonders' (see Micah 7:15)."

The student sitting next to me bolted out of his chair. "Rabbi! Rabbi! Does Rabbi Schneerson mean to say that the Meshiah will come this year?"

Without saying a word, the rabbi nodded his head. The en-tire room exploded. "Hurrah! *He is coming very soon!*" we all shouted together.

It was the most wonderful news I had ever received in my en-tire life. If I understood the rabbi correctly, it meant that Mashiah would arrive by the end of the current Jewish year—Rosh Hashanah, at the end of September. His coming was only three months away!

------

[1] Organized during the last decades of the eighteenth century by Rabbi Schneur Zalman, the author of the *Taniya*, this movement has a mystical interpretation of the Torah and emphasizes the soon coming of the Messiah. The yeshiva that I at-tended belonged to Lubavichers.

[2] A. E. Friedman, *From Exile to Redemption* (New York: Kenot Publication Society, 1992), p. 107.

[3] *Ibid.*

[4] *Ibid.*, p. 108.

[5] *Ibid.*, p. 7.

[6] According to the chronology of the Bible (Masoretic text), 1995/1996 is the 5,756th year from the creation of the world.

[7] Friedman, p. 20.

CHAPTER 21

BUT HE SAID,

YEA RATHER,

BLESSED ARE THEY

THAT HEAR

THE WORD OF GOD,

AND

KEEP IT.

—*Luke 11:28*

Excitement filled the synagogue. "The Mashiah is coming!" was on everybody's lips.

In anticipation of the great event, many people prepared to move to Israel, including my two closest friends at the synagogue—Chaim, with his wife, Esther, and Naphtali, with his entire family, including his parents, brothers and sisters, aunt, uncle, and cousins.

On July 25 our whole yeshiva group gathered at the main train station in Kiev to say goodbye to Chaim, Naphtali, and their *mishpahoth* ("families"). It was a sad day for me. The two guys were the only close friends I had at the yeshiva. They were the only ones I felt I could talk to and share with openly.

As I stood at the train station, Chaim came over and gave me a hug. "Be of good cheer," he said. "Mashiah is about to come. We will tell you immediately when He comes, and I am sure you will know instantly, because such events have never happened in the entire history of the world!"

I was sure Chaim was right. In just a few weeks we would see our Mashiah! It filled me with great hope and softened the blow of saying goodbye to my two friends.

Just days after Chaim and Naphtali left for Israel, tension really picked up in the Middle East as Saddam Hussein invaded Kuwait. Calling Iraq "Babylon" and himself "Nebuchadnezzar," he planned to rebuild a strong "Babylonian" empire.

At the synagogue we received another letter from Rabbi Schneerson: "The time of Mashiah is really at hand!" he wrote. No one doubted him. Iraqi rockets were aimed at Israel. We were sure it would be the time that Mashiah would deliver His people. I could easily picture the huge golden dome being blown off the Temple Mount in Jerusalem and the bricks of the mosque crumbling to pieces. Then I could see God's true people praying on the very place where the holy Temple once stood, instead of weeping at the Western Wall.

In all of this excitement I had not forgotten my Christian friends. I still continued going to their small group meetings in the dormitory. During one meeting I stood up and said, "My friends, some great eschatological events are taking place. Look at what the media is saying. Iraq is calling itself a 'New Babylon.' I am sure that something really big is going to happen in the world within the next few weeks."

At the end of the meeting I went with Tolik to the Wednesday night service at the Seventh-day Adventist church. I liked attending these services, where they often talked about the importance of the Sabbath. Also, I enjoyed visiting with the pastor, Sergei, and other friends there at the church.

As we were riding the bus to Yamskaya Ulitsa ("street") in Kiev, I turned to Tolik and said, "Listen, I have something important to tell you, but I didn't want to say it in front of our entire study group at the dormitory, because it's an issue between you and me."

"OK," Tolik said. "What is it?"

"You remember our conversation about Daniel 9—about the 70-week prophecy?"

"Yes."

"Well, I still don't have an answer to it, but Rabbi Schneerson is telling us that Mashiah is coming really, *really* soon. And one of our Jewish commentaries says that the time of Mashiah will be revealed when the king of Persia will provoke an Arabian king [Yalkut Shimoni, Vol. II, sec. 449].

"Look where Iraqi troops are headed. Aren't they going to Kuwait, in Arabia? This prophecy is being fulfilled! Give me a month, and before Rosh Hashanah I will see my Mashiah, and you will see that you were wrong! At least you will be able to ask Him if He's already been here! And I'm sure that He will be able to explain to us the meaning of this mysterious passage in Daniel 9."

Tolik just listened and smiled. I could see that he didn't believe me. But the more he didn't believe me, the more eager I was to see the day when Mashiah would come and I could jump into Tolik's room and say, "Look! You didn't believe me, but He has come! He is already in Jerusalem! Turn on your television and you will see the Mashiah with a huge crowd surrounding Him on the Temple Mount!"

A month rolled by. As Rosh Hashanah approached, my heart beat faster each day with anticipation of the great event. The situation in the Persian Gulf grew really tense. More rockets targeted Israel. The entire country was preparing to defend itself.

But where was Mashiah? Would He come today? tomorrow? or next week? The days raced by faster and faster. Just 10 days remained until Rosh Hashanah.

Every day I watched television, scanned the newspaper, and looked in my mailbox for any message from Naphtali or Chaim, but it appeared as though they had evaporated. Since that day we had said goodbye at the train station, I had not received any word from them. Had there been a train crash somewhere? Had they not made it to Israel? Why hadn't I heard anything from them?

The yeshiva and synagogue resembled a disturbed anthill because everybody was as excited as I was. Soon, very, *very* soon, we expected to see our Mashiah. One by one we counted down the evenings until the eve of Rosh Hashanah—nine, eight, seven, six, five, four, three, two, one!

Finally it came, the last day of the Jewish year 5750. That evening Rosh Hashanah, the Jewish New Year, would arrive.

It was impossible to concentrate in my classes at the university. I couldn't listen to the teacher. The only thing I could think about was the fact that *this* was the day Mashiah would arrive!

As soon as class was over at 3:00 p.m., I rushed to my room and turned on the television, expecting to hear something on the afternoon news about the Mashiah's arrival. But there was no news about Israel or the arrival of a Mashiah.

Slowly the afternoon hours crawled by as I waited. Soon it would be time to go to the synagogue for the Rosh Hashanah eve service. Surely the rabbi would make some announcement about the Mashiah's arrival.

At last it was time to attend synagogue. With the sun low on the horizon, I listened to the mournful sounds of the great shofar horn, ushering in the new year. "This will be a year of great wonders," Rabbi Schneerson had said, but where were these wonders now?

I had no idea that it would be my last Rosh Hashanah to celebrate. And I didn't realize it at the time, but it would indeed be a year of wonders after all.

CHAPTER 22

When the long-expected Mashiah did not come, I sank into a deep depression. It was the greatest disappointment I had ever experienced, worse than the disillusionment I had experienced with Communism, even more bitter than my rejection by MIPHE.

Days, then weeks, passed by in a blur. It was difficult to concentrate. Difficult to study. Difficult to function. The Mashiah had not come, and it was hard to see where life was leading me.

One day during this bleak time my Christian friend Oleg dropped by my room and invited me to go with him to another section of Kiev, where he needed to take care of some business. I was glad to go along and just enjoy his company. As we rode the bus, our conversation drifted into the usual topic—religion.

"It's interesting, Sasha, that you have never really explained to us how you take care of the problem of sin and atonement."

"Well," I replied, "now that the Temple is destroyed, the only way to make atonement for our sins is through sincere repentance."

"But what are you going to do with the book of Leviticus, which you follow closely?" Oleg opened his Bible to Leviticus 1:4 and read: "'And he shall lay his hand on the head of the burnt offering, that it may be accepted for him to make atonement on his behalf. And he shall slay the young bull before the Lord'" (NASB).

"Look," he said. "It's clear to me that in the time of the Jewish sanctuary, the sin goes from the person and is transferred onto the animal. This is the beginning of atonement. Then, every Day of Atonement, according to Leviticus 16, the sins of the whole nation, along with the blood, should go into the Most Holy Place and then get wiped out from there with the scapegoat. Is anything like this done today in the synagogue? As Christians, we transfer our sins onto Jesus Christ, but to whom do you transfer your sins?"

It was a difficult question for me. I had never considered the problem before and had no answer. It amazed me that Oleg knew so much about the sanctuary service and the doctrine of atonement found in the book of Leviticus. He seemed to have a better grasp of its significance than I did!

Finally I shared with Oleg the words from *Kol Nidre*—a special prayer that we sang at the synagogue every year on Yom Kippur:

"All vows and obligations and oaths and other expressions binding us to go in the path of justice, which we have vowed and bound ourselves by and have not honored, from the last Day of Atonement until this Day of Atonement whose coming is only for good, of all these we repent. They are absolved, remitted, redeemed, void, and annulled. They are neither binding nor in effect. Remit, O our Father who is in heaven, our debts to Thee and the sins of all Thy holy congregation. May our transgressions not be transgressions and may our debts to Thee no longer be such. Receive our prayers in mercy as atonement upon our souls."*

I had liked that the prayer made me feel as though my soul was clean, but now Oleg's question pointed out to me that it was not what the Torah outlined as the way to atonement.

We had no high priest, and we didn't offer any blood sacrifices—not even a pigeon! But it was clear that Leviticus required a blood sacrifice, and that sins were to be placed upon it.

However, I still needed to give some sort of answer to Oleg, so I again mentioned what Maimonides had said about becoming righteous by keeping the 613 mitzvoth and being sincerely repentant on Yom Kippur.

"I still don't understand how it can be that your Rabbi Maimonides is calling only for repentance, when this is clearly against what Leviticus says about needing a substitute for every kind of sin," Oleg persisted. "What is your substitute?"

It was really hard for me to face such difficult questions. I had expected Mashiah to solve all of these problems, but He had not arrived. When was He coming? I did not know.

In that desperate moment of my life, I suddenly blurted out to Oleg, "What is the essence of sin, Oleg? I mean in the Christian understanding, because for me sin has always been portrayed as the breaking of one of the 613 commandments. It has always been stressed that we should keep them, but what are we going to do if we miss keeping even one of them? The rabbi never explained that to us."

"Sin," Oleg answered, "in essence is the rejection of love. God sent His only Son that no one would perish, but that everyone would have eternal life. He did it out of love, and anyone who rejects it is a sinner.

"Love for and from your neighbor is also important. If you refuse to love your neighbor or accept his or her love, you are a sinner."

I had never heard such concepts before, and they gave me a lot to think about. While Oleg was doing his business, I kept mulling over what he had said: "Sin in essence is the rejection of love—God's love and your neighbor's love." It sure sounded different than trying to keep 613 mitzvoth.

On the way back to the university a question suddenly came bolting through my mind and out my mouth: "Oleg, do you think that I would ever become a Christian?"

He pondered my question for a few moments, as if searching for the right words. I could see his eyes filling with tears as he responded.

"We have been praying for you specifically every day. All of our study group. I know God loves you and that He wants to save you. And I know it will be really hard for Him to lose you."

My sarcasm vanished instantly. Seeing that Oleg was absolutely sincere, I couldn't believe that he cared so much about me that he thought about me and prayed for me *every day!* It was hard to resist that kind of love.

We parted at the dormitory. It was late in the evening, and I had a lot to think about. Oleg's words kept coming to my mind: "Sin is the rejection of God's love. Sin is the rejection of love for and from your neighbor."

My Christian friends loved me so much that they prayed for me every day. No one had loved me that much, except perhaps my own parents. Chaim, Naphtali, Chaika, and Ilyia were good friends, but I realized that I had never been so close to them that I had been a part of their everyday thoughts, nor had I expected it from them.

Nor had I expected it from my Christian friends. But whether I had expected it or not, it existed, and it could not leave my heart untouched.

---

*The High Holiday CD, *Beth Hatefutsith* (1984); English by Amatsya Arnon.

CHAPTER 23

MY FATHER,

WHICH GAVE THEM ME,

IS GREATER

THAN ALL;

AND NO MAN IS ABLE

TO PLUCK THEM

OUT OF

MY FATHER'S HAND.

—*John 10:29*

Even though it was one of the few quiet nights in my room—no loud music, no smell of cigarettes and vodka, because Chaika was out of town—I still had trouble sleeping.

My mind churned with heavy questions: What do I have in my life? What kind of future will it be? Will Mashiah ever come? And if He doesn't, what or whom am I expecting? What reasons do I have right now for not believing the prophecy in Daniel 9?

I had been expecting Mashiah to resolve these difficult passages, but what if He didn't come? Who would give me an explanation? And did an alternative explanation even exist when the text seemed to so clearly indicate that the Mashiah would be put to death *before* the destruction of the Temple?

But how could it be that for so many centuries such great rabbis as Rashi, Maimonides, and others could not discover the meaning of Daniel 9? How could it be that the Talmud did not give a word of explanation on it? And in fact, instead of commenting on the passage, it pronounced a curse only upon anyone who would attempt to calculate the 70 weeks. Were they trying to hide something? And why was it forbidden to read Isaiah 53 in the synagogue?

On the other hand, it was easy to see why Maimonides and the other rabbis of the Middle Ages would have a difficult time believing that Christ was the Messiah when people who called themselves Christians were massacring Jews and others in the name of Christ. I had read in the yeshiva library that Rashi used to believe that the suffering servant in Isaiah 53 was to be the Mashiah, but after the Crusades he purposely changed his mind.* I could understand why.

On the other hand, the Christian group called Seventh-day Adventists had a clear and logical message. They said that many of the Christian churches had apostatized from the first apostolic movement. I could see that it was true. All the apostles were Jews. And I had read for myself that the New Testament did not reject the law, including the Sabbath.

I remembered my various conversations with Tolik and Oleg that had raised important questions about sin and the atonement. Such questions were now screaming in my mind—*What am I going to do? How can I ever make atonement for my sins? Shall I climb to the roof of the dormitory, capture a couple pigeons, and sacrifice them as a sin offering? That seems crazy, but if I don't do it, who will bear all my sins? Isaiah 53 says that the suffering servant can do it, but if I don't accept this suffering servant as my Mashiah, what am I going to do with my sins?*

Oleg's arguments were right. The *Kol Nidre* prayer that we sang every Yom Kippur really didn't help solve the sin problem. It seemed like a kind of ritual I went through that satisfied my feelings but not reality. Did the *Kol Nidre* prayer really remove our sins? Did it really do all that the Torah required us to do? If not, then I had been an unforgiven sinner for many years and desperately needed *Someone* to take my sins away.

What if Christ really is the Mashiah? I wondered. *And what if I accept Him? What will the other students at the yeshiva think of me? I will be a traitor—the worst thing a Jew could ever be. They'll call me a* vykrest—*a Jew who has been baptized into the Christian church.* Vykrest was a word full of shame. We were told that the vykrests were always our worst enemies—even worse than the Jesuits or the Inquisition.

As I continued wrestling with these seemingly unanswerable questions, another voice suddenly began to speak louder than my own thoughts: "Weigh all of the pros and cons. What is more important to you—to have atonement for your sins or not to be called a traitor? And even after you accept Christ as the Mashiah, it doesn't mean that you are turning your back on Judaism. You are not going to go back to the synagogue and try to do something mean and revengeful. That is not your purpose at all. Whom are you going to hurt by accepting Christ? Are you going to injure the rabbi? Chaim? How is your decision going to damage the synagogue?"

The voice continued, "Your decision is your personal business. It is not anyone else's business. And by your decision you are not going to harm anyone else. You don't have any malicious plans toward anyone. In reality you're not going to hurt anybody. *But if you don't accept Christ and your sins are not remitted, isn't that going to injure you? Even if you find out later that Christ is not the Mashiah, what have you lost by accepting Him now?"*

The voice's arguments were reasonable and powerful. There was nothing more that could be said. I had to make a decision, so I made it and fell into a calm sleep.

I woke up two hours later, feeling completely well rested and refreshed. Quickly dressing, I hurried down to the little room where I knew Oleg and my other Christian friends met for prayer each morning at 7:00.

As I stepped into the room, I could see surprise on my friends' faces. I had never attended their early-morning prayer meetings, since the only thing they did then was pray to Jesus.

"What brings you here so early this morning?" Oleg asked me.

"I accepted Him."

Oleg, Nicholai, Tolik, and the others looked at one another but didn't say anything.

"I accepted Him," I repeated.

Oleg and Tolik stared at me and finally with trembling voices asked together, "You mean Christ?"

"Yes." I could see how happy they were.

"Would you like to pray to Jesus with us?" Oleg asked.

"Yes," I replied.

So Oleg prayed. "Dear Jesus, thank You for sending the Holy Spirit to Sasha, and for bringing him to the truth of Your Word, and for his acceptance of You as his Saviour and Redeemer. Amen."

As Oleg prayed, it was the first time that the name of Christ did not cause a shivering sensation down my spine. I really felt that I had become good friends with Him and was sure that I would never be sorry for the decision I had made that night.

---

*Charles E. McLain, "A Comparison of Ancient and Medieval Jewish Interpretations of the Suffering Servant in Isaiah," *Calvary Baptist Theological Journal,* Fall 1990.

CHAPTER 24

BUT IN VAIN

THEY DO

WORSHIP ME,

TEACHING

FOR DOCTRINES

THE COMMANDMENTS

OF MEN.

—*Matthew 15:9*

Now that I had accepted Christ as my Mashiah, I faced another problem—what was I going to do about my studies at the yeshiva? Close to completing all of the work necessary to receive a diploma, I just needed a few more weeks of study.

Not knowing what the future might bring, I thought that the document might be important. Maybe I would need it for something someday. I didn't know. Besides, after already having completed so much study, including Hebrew, it would be a shame just to let it go to waste.

On the other hand, how in the world could I continue at the yeshiva and attend the synagogue after having accepted Christ as Mashiah? I didn't want to be a hypocrite.

Fortunately, during the month of November the yeshiva had no classes, so I didn't have to face the problem immediately.

Before too long, however, it was mid-December and time for Hanukkah.

I knew the other yeshiva students would be looking for me to attend the special service. And I had heard that a new rabbi had come from America. Thinking that it would be interesting to see what was going on, as well as to get a look at the new rabbi, I decided to go.

The weather was really bad. Wet, mushy snow covered the ground, and the roads were slick. Leaving the metro station, I carefully but quickly picked my way through the slush. Since it was cold, I wanted to cover the mile from the metro to the synagogue as quickly as possible.

Arriving at last at the iron gates of the synagogue, I was surprised to find about 200 people shivering in the cold, waiting for the door to open. It was less than an hour before sundown, and I couldn't understand why the synagogue's doors were still locked.

"Is the rabbi here?" I asked the guard at the gate.

"Yes, he's inside," the guard nodded. "He hasn't found an apartment yet, so he's temporarily living in the guest room near his office. I haven't seen him come out this afternoon, so I'm sure he's in there."

This is strange, I thought. *Why in the world isn't the rabbi opening the doors? The weather is terrible, and the people are freezing out here.*

And where is Abramovich, the senior cantor? I wondered. *He also has a key to the synagogue, and he surely must be coming. Isn't this Hanukkah?*

Trying to keep warm, I stuck my hands into my coat pockets. Suddenly I felt something in my right-hand pocket. It was a key to the door that led down to the library book depository in the basement of the synagogue! When Chaim had left for Israel, he had given me the key, asking that I return it to the rabbi. But somehow I had forgotten about it.

I decided to use the key to get in and try to find the rabbi so I could ask him to open the doors for the people. Stepping inside the little corridor, I could hear voices coming from the basement. As I quickly went down the stairs, they grew louder.

"I think Stolichnaya vodka is more kosher than Russkaya," said a voice I did not recognize.

"But what about Pshenichnaya vodka?" said another voice I knew for sure was Abramovich's. "I think it's more kosher than any of the others."

I could hear laughter from behind the door. Peeking in through the keyhole, I saw Abramovich sitting at a small table with another man dressed in a rabbinical *lopserdockst. So this must be the new rabbi!* I concluded.

As disturbing as the conversation was, what I saw on the table made me feel even sicker. In addition to a large bottle of vodka sat a huge chunk of Ukrainian lard beside some bread. I could see the new rabbi eating his lard sandwich.

"What a sacrilege!" I said to myself. "Am I actually going to stay for the service?" With the speed of a bullet I ran out the door, threw the key on the ground, and said to myself, "This is God's answer. He probably doesn't see any sense in my graduating from this yeshiva!"

CHAPTER 25

Although I had accepted Jesus Christ as my Saviour and was no longer going to the yeshiva, I was still afraid to be baptized. I didn't want to be called a vykrest. However, I continued attending the Seventh-day Adventist church on Yamskaya Street every Sabbath, and I enjoyed spending time with my Christian friends, especially Tolik.

Tolik attended church every Sabbath, and each Sunday he went to another church in Kiev called the "New Life Center," where he worked as a translator.

This New Life Center, which had just opened in 1990, was a multidenominational evangelical church. In addition, it served as a base for American evangelical missionaries coming to work in the Soviet Union. Since few people in the U.S.S.R. knew English, everyone desperately needed translators.

I admired Tolik's English ability and wished that I could speak English too. I had studied English grammar for years in Soviet schools, but could hardly speak a word of the language. Hoping Tolik could help me learn to speak English, I asked him about it. "Oh, it isn't difficult," he said. "You've studied English for years—I went through this same torture too. But now I can speak English because I practice communicating with it. Why don't you come to New Life with me this Sunday? There'll be a whole group of Americans there, and you'll have lots of opportunities to practice speaking English." Delighted, I agreed to accompany Tolik to the New Life Center the following week.

After arriving at the center, we were introduced to a large group of American high school students, along with their teacher, Greg Gregory. They were the first Americans I had ever met.

"My name is Sasha," I said in my best English. Excitedly the American teenagers surrounded me and started speaking rapidly. I didn't have a clue as to what they were saying, but desperately wanted to be able to communicate with them.

The experience gave me powerful motivation to learn English. I started private English lessons and went each Sunday to the New Life Center with Tolik, where the service was held in both English and Russian. My conversational ability grew quickly, and each week I could communicate more and more with the American missionaries.

While I enjoyed visiting with these various Christian missionaries, something troubled me. I had met American Baptists, Pentecostals, Presbyterians, and various other denominations, but had yet to encounter any Seventh-day Adventist missionaries. *Did the Seventh-day Adventist Church not exist in America? Was the Seventh-day Adventist church on Yamskaya Street the only Adventist church in the world?* I wondered.

I really felt comfortable at the Adventist church, and I could see that they based their doctrines soundly on the Bible. But what a pity if the only Seventh-day Adventists in all the world were just here in Kiev!

One Sabbath I decided to broach the subject with Pastor Yuri. "Well," he said, "there are approximately 7 million Seventh-day Adventists in the world. And moreover, the Seventh-day Adventist Church is one of the most widespread churches in the world. We believe in the principle that Jesus outlined in Matthew 24:14: 'And this gospel of the kingdom will be preached in all the world as a witness to all the nations, and then the end will come' [NKJV].

"God wants His law and His gospel to be known all around the world. Even in the Old Testament Isaiah wrote: 'My house shall be called a house of prayer for all nations' [Isa. 56:7, NKJV]. So we believe that we should spread this message around the world.

"Our church is responding to that call of God, and it has its representatives in more than 200 countries around the globe—it is the second most widespread denomination in the world.

"By the way," the pastor continued, "an American preacher is arriving this Tuesday to hold some meetings here in Kiev. You are welcome to come, and if you would like to talk with this man, I think I can arrange it."

Pastor Yuri handed me a small brochure advertising the meetings: "Pastor John Robert Spangler invites you to come to the House of Organ Music to study the Bible—Let's Get Acquainted With Jesus Together." It looked appealing, and I decided that I would go.

The following Wednesday I made my way to the beautiful House of Organ Music. Originally built as a Roman Catholic church in the nineteenth century, since 1927 it had served as a magnificent place for organ and other musical concerts. Pastor Spangler's meetings were the first religious meetings to be held in the building since 1927, when it had still functioned as a Catholic church.

Spangler immediately impressed me. He was composed, his

biblical presentations were clear and logical, and I could see that he was an intelligent person. What a joy it was to come night after night and listen to the wonderful sermons. I loved how he blended the Old and New Testaments, accepting the entire Bible, not just the New Testament, as the Word of God.

Although the series of meetings lasted only five nights, by the end I felt impressed that I needed to make a more public and definite commitment to Jesus Christ. I wanted to talk to Pastor Spangler personally, so after the final meeting on Sunday evening, I went up to the stage. A car was waiting for Pastor Spangler, and I could see that he was about to leave.

Hurriedly I went over to Pastor Yuri, who was standing near the stage, and asked him if I could talk with Pastor Spangler. He said I could and inquired if I needed a translator. I decided that I wanted to try to speak to the American preacher myself without a translator, so I quickly walked over to him.

"Pastor Spangler," I began, "I am Jewish, and I recently came to the conclusion that Jesus Christ is my Messiah."

The man's eyes widened. He probably hadn't expected me to say this. I could see that he was listening carefully, and it gave me courage to continue. "But here is a strange thing. When I came to the Christians, I saw so many different denominations, all believing that Christ is the Messiah, and I really don't know which church I should join."

"Well," Spangler replied, "you have to join the church that really follows the Bible."

His answer did not satisfy me.

"Pastor Spangler, I know I shouldn't go to the Catholic Church, which just follows tradition, but all the other churches claim they follow the Bible and the Bible alone."

Spangler could probably sense that it is not easy to deal with me, so he asked, "Since you are Jewish, now that you have come to Christ, do you believe that the Ten Commandments, including the Sabbath, are still valid and should be kept?"

"Yes," I replied. "I read in Hebrews where the apostle Paul says that for the people of God a Sabbath rest remains."

Then Spangler asked me another question: "Do you know of any church that keeps the Sabbath?"

"Well, I'm not really that experienced in Christianity," I said. "I know that here in Kiev there is a Seventh-day Adventist church that observes the Sabbath, and I also have met a lot of Americans who have come to Kiev through the New Life Center, and they do not keep the Sabbath. But I don't know if any other church in the world besides the Adventists honors the Sabbath."

"The Seventh-day Adventist Church does not exist only in Kiev," Spangler said. "It's a worldwide church, which all around the world keeps the same Ten Commandments and the same Sabbath. I personally do not know of any other church in the world that adheres to these same principles. The Seventh-day Adventist Church gives this message to all nations of the world, including the Jews, so it has this message for you, too. And I can see that you believe in this message, so I don't know what more I should say to you."

As I left the meeting hall that night I was so excited that I could hardly contain myself. Here was a worldwide church that believed in Jesus Christ as the Messiah, and also still believed in the Ten Commandments, including the Sabbath.

Eagerly I waited in front of the church for Pastor Yuri. Soon he came around the corner, and we walked together to the metro station. Nervous and hesitant, for a while I just talked about casual things, but finally I took a deep breath and asked, "Yuri Grigoriyevich, how can I become a member of the Seventh-day Adventist Church?"

I could see that my question pleased him, and he replied,

"Keep attending the church services regularly. Your decision is a very serious one, and you need to know where you're going. If you will stay after the church service for the special Bible studies, you will learn all the doctrines of the church. There is a baptism scheduled for June 22."

I decided that June 22, 1991, was going to be a very special day for me, and determined in my heart that nothing would prevent me from being baptized.

CHAPTER 26

BUT OF THAT DAY

AND HOUR

KNOWETH NO MAN,

NO, NOT

THE ANGELS OF HEAVEN,

BUT MY FATHER

ONLY.

—Matthew 24:36

Although I was planning to be baptized into the Seventh-day Adventist Church, I still went to the New Life Center each Sunday with Tolik in order to practice my English.

One Sunday a girl at the New Life Center came up to me and asked if I would like to meet another Jewish Christian. Would I? I was ecstatic! I didn't know that any other Jewish Christians even existed.

That afternoon she took me to the Dnieper Hotel in Kiev, where the American missionaries were staying, and introduced me to Jeff Kipp. Jeff was from Minneapolis, Minnesota, and was working with an organization called "Good News for Israel."

He was happy to meet me, and we became good friends almost instantly. My English was fairly fluent by this time, and so during the next several days we spent a lot of time together, talking, sightseeing around Kiev, and visiting with other Jews.

Then Friday arrived. Jeff and I had

spent another enjoyable day together, but now it was late afternoon, and soon it would be time for the Friday evening vespers service. "Jeff," I said, "the Sabbath is coming. I need to go to church."

"What?" His face turned green. "Which Sabbath are you talking about? Are you telling me that you are connected with the
Seventh-day Adventists? If you want to be a real Messianic Jew,
stay away from them.

"There are many other churches you can join. I myself am
charismatic. I don't force you to speak in tongues, but if you want
to, I can teach you how. But please, please, if you want to hear the
experience of a good Jew, don't ever go to the Adventist Church."

Stunned, I couldn't understand why a fellow Jewish Christian
was so vehement against the Adventist Church. "Why are you so
against the Adventist Church?" I asked. "I'm studying the Bible
with them and even planning to be baptized in a couple months."

At this Jeff went crazy. "They're legalists and don't believe in
grace! Adventists believe everybody is saved by the law!" Excited,
he spoke so fast that I couldn't understand him.

This guy isn't making any sense at all! I thought to myself. I realized from my own reading of the Bible as well as from the Bible
studies I was taking at the local Adventist church that Jeff didn't
know what he was talking about.

In fact, just during that week's Bible study the pastor had
shared with us the Adventist view of salvation and grace: "Led
by the Holy Spirit we sense our need, acknowledge our sinful-
ness, repent of our transgressions, and exercise faith in Jesus as
Lord and Christ, as Substitute and Example. This faith which receives salvation comes through the divine power of the Word
and is the gift of God's grace."*

I went to church that Friday evening not bothered by Jeff's arguments. Instead I believed the apostle Paul when he wrote to the
Hebrews that there still remained a "Sabbath rest for the people of

God." He had never written a word about changing the day of worship for Jews or Gentiles, and he himself had worshiped on the Sabbath.

However, although I disagreed with Jeff on his view of Adventists, I still enjoyed his friendship and company. So the next day, after the Sabbath evening service, I went back to his hotel room.

He was excited to see me. "I know how to convince you that the Seventh-day Adventist Church is not the right church," he said. "I will take you to Minneapolis for the Congress of Messianic Jews, and I will baptize you there in August.

"You just haven't seen any good alternatives to the Adventist Church," he continued. "There aren't many Jews here in Russia with whom you can share your experience, but in Minneapolis you will see many Jews, and we will prove to you that you are not going the right way. Believe me, there is not a single Jew in the Seventh-day Adventist Church, as long as *you* don't go there!" he said, pointing his finger at my chest. He was lying about no Jews belonging to the Adventist Church, but I didn't realize it at the time.

Although nothing in the world was going to stop me from being baptized into the Seventh-day Adventist Church on June 22, Jeff's offer of a free trip to America was irresistible. My Adventist friend Tolik was going to the States to study at a college there. Here was my golden opportunity.

Jeff handed me an official letter of invitation through the New Life Center and 18,000 rubles (the equivalent of $600 at the time) to buy an Aeroflot ticket to Minneapolis. It was more money than I had ever seen in my wildest dreams. With such a sum one could buy a small house in the Ukrainian countryside.

It seemed that my life was finally coming together. I had found the true church, plus a ticket to America. Who could ask for more?

Seventh-day Adventists Believe . . . A Biblical Exposition of 27 Fundamental Doctrines (Hagerstown, Md.: Review and Herald Pub. Assn., 1988), p. 118.

CHAPTER 27

BUT SANCTIFY

THE LORD GOD

IN YOUR HEARTS:

AND BE READY ALWAYS

TO GIVE AN ANSWER

TO EVERY MAN

THAT ASKETH YOU

A REASON OF THE HOPE

THAT IS IN YOU

WITH MEEKNESS

AND FEAR.

—1 Peter 3:15

The words of Pastor Spangler continued to echo through my mind as I prepared for baptism: "The Seventh-day Adventist Church has a message for all nations and welcomes everybody." It strongly appealed to me, and I eagerly looked forward to the time when I would be baptized into this church.

At last Sabbath, June 22, arrived. I listened excitedly as the elder made a special announcement at the beginning of the church service:

"Dear brothers and sisters, tomorrow we will have a very joyful event. God is good to us. We will have the first baptism in the city of Kiev that has been officially allowed to be held in public. We no longer need to hide.

"More than 70 people are waiting for the opportunity to make a covenant with Jesus Christ, and our little baptistry is just too small. So we have been given permission to hold the baptism in the Dnieper River.

"This is the first time in history

that we have been able to do this openly, and anyone who wishes is welcome to see this sacred ceremony.

"We congratulate all of our baptismal candidates on their decision and want to invite everyone who is able to come and support them during this solemn moment in their lives."

Then turning to the candidates, he said to us: "We would like to invite you, dear candidates, to stay for a little while after the church service so that we can personally review with you everything we have studied during our Bible classes and see if you have any questions prior to your baptism."

My heart filled with happiness during the entire church service, knowing that tomorrow I was going to be baptized!

After the service I, along with the other candidates, went into another room while we waited to meet with the pastor and church board. There I noticed Alexei Antonovich, a retired pastor who sometimes preached when Pastor Yuri was away, speaking with a young woman who looked to be about 17. She was wearing a white blouse and blue plaid skirt. Guessing that she also was planning on being baptized the next day, I went over to where she and Alexei Antonovich were standing.

"Irina," said Pastor Alexei, "this is our brother Sasha. He is also going to be baptized." Then turning to me, he asked, "Sasha, when is your turn to go into the boardroom?"

"I think in about five minutes," I responded.

"Would you mind if Irina went ahead of you?" he asked.

I didn't mind. *Where is this girl from?* I wondered. I had never seen her before. Standing a little distance from where she and Pastor Alexei were talking, I could overhear a bit of their conversation. It seemed that Irina's parents were not at all happy about her decision to be baptized. Her mother was an Orthodox Christian and her father a staunch atheist.

Soon Irina entered the boardroom. I waited by the door so that

I would be next. After a few minutes she came out, and her face did not look happy. I wondered what the problem was. My turn was next.

As I walked into the room, Pastor Yuri introduced me to the elders and said, "Alexander is Jewish, and I am sure he has no questions about the Sabbath or clean and unclean foods." Then we went over the fundamental beliefs of the Adventist Church, all of which I believed. The church board asked me a few questions about myself—where I lived, what I did, etc. After a few minutes they congratulated me about my decision to be baptized and said, "We'll see you tomorrow."

When I returned to the other room, I saw Pastor Alexei talking to Irina, who was crying. "You have to go back in there," he was saying. "Even though you don't know some of the doctrines yet, you must tell them that you will attend the Bible studies regularly, and that you love God and you want to make a covenant with Him and that you plan to do everything that is according to His will."

While Irina was back in the boardroom, Pastor Alexei explained to me that she had come to the church for the first time just one month earlier. The pastor did not really know her and had recommended that she wait until the next baptism.

"Wow," I said to him, "one month is not a lot of time to become acquainted with all of the Bible doctrines." I had been attending church for nearly five months and was still learning, so how much could she know?

"Well," Alexei Antonovich said, "I have been studying with her for the past 10 days, and she has been very open to everything, accepting all of the doctrines that we have studied. She needs to find God, and they cannot refuse her baptism if she sincerely loves the Lord and wants to make a covenant with Him. So I told her to go back and tell them all of this and not to be afraid. They cannot refuse."

We could see from the smile on her face when she came out of the boardroom that she would be among those baptized the next day.

June 23, 1991, began with a bang—thunder, lightning, and heavy rain that seemed to intensify every minute. *Well,* I thought, *how are they going to do the baptism in this kind of weather?* I hoped they wouldn't cancel it.

The baptism was scheduled to be held on the far north edge of Kiev. Since Kiev State University was located on the south side, I needed to allow plenty of time in order to reach the baptism site. First I took the bus to the metro, then rode the metro to the end of the line. From there I took another bus across a bridge to an island right in the middle of the Dnieper River.

It was the site of the baptism. To my happiness and relief, I saw many people heading toward the large beach that the church had rented for this special event. So the baptism wasn't canceled after all!

And it seemed that God had worked a special miracle in our behalf. While rain poured down all over Kiev, and black storm clouds blanketed the sky, a large hole in the clouds hovered directly above the island. We looked up into the clear blue sky and enjoyed the warmth of the sunshine while the rest of Kiev was getting soaked!

The crowd gathered together while the baptismal candidates went into special tents to change. I put on a pair of white pants along with a white shirt and jacket. The women received white robes to wear and scarves for their heads.

Leaving the dressing tents, we gathered together beside the river and listened to a brass band play and a choir sing Russian and Ukrainian hymns. It was beautiful to listen to this heavenly music and see the sun sparkling on the river.

When the music finished, an older pastor, who I later learned was the secretary of the newly organized Ukrainian Union of the Seventh-day Adventist Church in the U.S.S.R., began to preach.

Standing at the water's edge, he explained to the crowd the meaning of baptism. And to the candidates he spoke words of encouragement and affirmation of the important step we were taking. For most of the people it was the first time that they had ever witnessed baptism by full immersion.

After about a half hour, five pastors stepped into the water, wearing large baptismal robes. Following the pastors were the first five of the 70 baptismal candidates. Each pastor raised his right hand above the baptismal candidate while the union secretary on the shore also raised his hand and said, "*Vo hemeya Otsah, Syna, e Svaytovo Dukha, Kreschu Vas. Amein.*"* Then all together the pastors gently lowered the candidates completely under the water and up again.

The pastors repeated the process again and again, five candidates at a time. I was in the fifth group. Stepping into the water, I went straight toward Pastor Yuri Grigoriyevich, who was one of the baptizing ministers. Glancing to the side, I noticed that Irina, the girl I had met the previous day at church, happened to be in the same group I was in. She was heading toward Pastor Alexei Antonovich, who was also baptizing. The pastors raised their hands, and then we were all baptized in the Dnieper River. It was a very special moment in my life.

As soon as the last of the 70 candidates came up out of the water, the blue hole in the sky above the island closed up and rain began to pour. We quickly changed our clothes, gathered up our things, and ran toward the bus stop. As we raced along, I saw my good Adventist friend Sergei, whom I had met the previous year in Tolik's room.

Sergei called out to me, "Let's go to my place. I'll introduce you to my brother." We took the bus back into Kiev together, and by the time we arrived at Sergei's apartment, we were drenched.

Vitaly, Sergei's brother, waited for us. He also was a Seventh-day Adventist, and in fact was studying at the newly opened seminary in Zaokski, Russia. I was interested to hear about the school, the first Protestant seminary ever to open in the history of Russia or the U.S.S.R. Vitaly was in its very first class and had just completed his second year.

He wanted to know all about me—my Jewish background and how I had accepted Christ. Toward the end of the visit he said, "I'm sure our seminary president will be very interested to hear about you. Maybe you'll be invited to come to the seminary someday."

That's nice, I thought, *but I don't need the seminary. The plane to America is waiting for me.*

---

*"In the name of the Father, Son, and Holy Ghost I baptize you. Amen."

CHAPTER 28

The plane may have been waiting to take me to America, but the KGB was definitely not in a hurry to let me go. While every Soviet citizen had to have an internal passport* for use within their own country, getting an international passport was another matter.

The process is long and complicated. First of all, one must go to the local OVIR office—the government bureaucracy that grants exit visas giving permission to leave the country as well as international passports. There one stands in line, literally, for about 10 days. Of course, the poor applicant goes home at night, but returns the next morning to claim his or her place in line. At last the day arrives when you can present your application for an international passport. It then goes on to the KGB, where it sits for about five months while they check all their records on the applicant. If the person passes this scrutiny, he or she receives an international passport and can leave the country.

Applying for an international passport to visit one of the Eastern Bloc countries, such as Poland, usually doesn't take too long. However, to visit a Western country, particularly the United States, the procedure can be lengthy and rigorous.

I had started as soon as I had received the official letter of invitation from Jeff, but as the weeks ticked by, I grew more and more nervous. Every week I checked with a friend who worked at the OVIR office, and each time he would tell me, "Oh, your passport is still at the KGB." I was becoming worried, because I had poured almost all of my heart into this great desire to go to America.

During this time I continued attending the Adventist church on Yamskaya Street each Sabbath, as well as the midweek meeting on Wednesday and Friday evening vespers. In addition, I attended the prayer meetings held each morning at the New Life Center.

The morning meetings offered special prayers for many people who were having similar troubles obtaining their international passports. We prayed for them, and their problems resolved, but mine did not. In fact, their success increased my worry.

I couldn't understand why God did not answer the prayers about my passport difficulties when it seemed that He took care of everyone else's problems. As July rolled by, I became more and more anxious. I was supposed to be in Minneapolis by August 3.

One morning after the prayer service at the New Life Center a young man named Igor approached me. I had never talked to him about my passport problems, but he came over to me and said, "Brother, I have a message for you. God has revealed to me that everything will be well with you. You will get your passport at the very last moment. God just wants to test your patience, but in order to pass the test, you need to understand something. God wants you to be filled with the Holy Spirit. If you will open your heart to God, He will pour out His Holy Spirit upon you, and He will bless you."

I knew what he meant about being "filled with the Holy Spirit"—speaking the kind of nonsense I had heard when I visited the Pentecostal church. *What a farce!* I thought to myself. *To speak this crazy glossolalia. Impossible. I can't act like that!*

But as the days passed and my passport remained lost somewhere in the labyrinth of the KGB, I grew desperate. Everyone else at the prayer meetings was getting their passports—everyone except me. Could it be that I was not doing something right? What was the problem?

Really wanting to go to America, I began to wonder if maybe there was something to the concept of speaking in tongues. Although I didn't know many biblical arguments against it at the time, the idea of actually doing it seemed ugly to me. But I was desperate. I needed to get a passport.

So exactly one week before my flight was scheduled to leave for America I decided it was time to do something drastic. After the morning prayer meeting at the New Life Center, I went up to Valari, one of the assistant directors, and asked him how I could get the gift of tongues.

"Well," he said, "that's very easy. You just have to pray earnestly and God will send it to you. Let's pray just now."

So we knelt, and Valari began: "O Lord, heavenly Father, You know the earnest desire of Brother Sasha to receive Your Holy Spirit. Please send it to him. Please empower him with the words of Your heavenly tongue . . ." Then he really took off and slipped into what seemed like gibberish to me.

I just stayed on my knees while Valari continued his prayer, but nothing came out of my own mouth. Finally Valari said, "Amen!" Then looking up at me, he asked, "Did it happen to you?"

"Did what happen?" I asked.

"The tongues! Didn't the Holy Spirit come upon you during my prayer?" he asked incredulously. "It shouldn't be like this. God gives this gift to everybody, especially after the earnest prayer of your brother. You probably aren't opening your heart wide enough to receive it."

"How can I not be opening my heart?" I asked. "I really want it. It's just that it isn't coming."

"Well," Valari said, "I can see that you are sincere. I think that maybe the problem is just that your flesh tongue isn't used to this kind of movement, so let's try this. In order to make God's work easier, I'll just pray in tongues, and while I'm doing that, you just repeat over and over, 'Jesus, I love You.'"

So he began to pray in tongues again, and I started repeating, "Jesus, I love You . . . Jesus, I love You . . . Jesus, I love You . . . Jesus . . ." I was to continue the phrase over and over as long as Valari kept praying. After about 30 minutes my tongue began to feel like a piece of raw meat flapping around in my mouth, and it began to rebel by making strange sounds of its own.

When Valari heard the noises I was making, he exclaimed, "Hallelujah! You've got it! Now you are blessed! I believe that God will do what He has promised to do.

"By the way," he added, "I also have the gift of prophecy. And during my prayer God revealed to me that you will be really blessed. You will get to the States, and you will be able to get into a good American college, and then in five years you will come back and will pastor a great church." After this "prophecy" my soul calmed down somewhat, and I left the New Life Center with the assurance that I would get to the States.

Although I still did not have my international passport, I decided to go to the Aeroflot agency to purchase my tickets, since I was catching a train that night for Kuznetsovsk to say goodbye to my parents.

By the time I reached the Aeroflot office an hour later, I was not feeling well. It felt as if I had a fever and was getting hotter all the time. I wished I could find somebody who could pray for my healing, but there was no one around who could help. Despite my sickness, I stood in line for two hours and finally purchased the coveted tickets to Minneapolis.

But I grew worse by the moment. By the time I boarded the train at 11:00 that night I was really ill. I lay down on the narrow bed and somehow fell into a restless sleep. At 4:00 a.m. I woke up with a strange, piercing pain in my chest that kept growing stronger and stronger. The pain was so bad I could no longer lie down. It was so severe that I wanted to climb the walls.

When the train stopped at Kuznetsovsk at 6:00 a.m. I somehow managed to stumble off it. Since it was too early to catch a bus, I miraculously managed to walk the three miles to my parents'.

When I arrived home, I was nearly unconscious. My mother didn't realize how much pain I was in, and said, "You must just be tired. Probably you have a fever, but it's not a big deal. You just need to get some good sleep." She gave me a special herb tea to help me rest.

I fell asleep for about three hours, then woke up screaming from the pain in my chest. My mother called the ambulance. Medics quickly came and took me to the hospital. Forty minutes after the cardiogram the results were in: "extensive myocardial infarction."

As I slipped in and out of consciousness, I realized that my "America Plan" had crashed. I knew now that it didn't matter whether I had an international passport or not—I wouldn't be going anywhere for a long time.

My mother was even more distraught than I was. Standing beside my hospital bed, she said, "Look what your God has done to you. You have been associating with these crazy believers, and now you're going to die."

Her words cut me deeply, but somehow in my state of semiconsciousness I managed to reply, "God brought me to this bed, and God is going to take care of me."

I began to pray as I had never done before. As I drifted in and out of consciousness because of all the pain medication I was receiving, my prayer lasted more than two hours because my thoughts each time would pick up where they left off before. For the first time in my life I really felt the hand of God holding me up. I realized how wrong I had been to trust in so-called prophets, and to try to push my own desires over the will of the Almighty.

James 1:13, 14 came to my mind as I was lying in the hospital: "Let no one say when he is tempted, 'I am tempted by God'; for God cannot be tempted by evil, nor does He Himself tempt anyone. But each one is tempted when he is drawn away by his own desires and enticed" (NKJV).

Right then and there in my hospital bed I poured out my heart to God, sincerely repenting for my sins and giving my entire being to Him. I felt at peace and had the assurance that my life was totally and absolutely in God's hands.

Ten days after I was admitted to the hospital, I began to feel some of my strength returning. But I still didn't know what kind of life I would be able to live. Would I ever be able to get out of the hospital bed? Would I be able to return to my studies at Kiev State University? I did not know the answers to my questions, but I did know for sure that God was with me.

Soon the doctor came in with the portable cardiograph machine. Every morning she did the same procedure, checking the condition of my heart. But this morning something was different. As she watched the monitor, her eyes became wider and wider. Without saying a word she repeated the procedure, something she had never done before. Then she went through it a third time. I wondered what the problem was. Finally she asked, "Where was the infarction? I can't believe my eyes! Two days ago this same machine was showing me that one fourth of your heart was totally dead. Now I don't see any major problems. You have just a small infection—pericarditis. This is unbelievable! I've never seen anything like this in my practice before."

I knew the answer. I knew that God had heard my prayer of repentance and had stepped in. Now I determined that after I got out of the hospital I would never again try to do anything that would contradict His will. I wanted to follow Him completely and totally in my life. I wanted to work for Him. Wherever He would send me, I was willing to go. I had become a true believer.

---

*The internal passport was and is the primary legal document used in the countries of the former Soviet Union. It contains personal information as well as the *propiska* registration that indicates what city the citizen is allowed to live and work in.

EPILOGUE

After recovering from his heart attack, Alexander continued his studies. In November 1991, while still studying at Kiev State, he enrolled in the extension program of Zaokski Theological Seminary. After he attended the program's ministerial classes, his desire to enter the ministry grew stronger.

The Ukrainian Union Conference asked him to be an evangelist-translator in August 1992. That September and October Sasha worked with three evangelists from the United States, two from Canada, and one from Brazil.

In January 1993 Alexander married Irina, the young woman he had met the evening before his baptism. After their marriage she traveled with Sasha to an evangelistic series in which she worked in the children's programs.

During the summer of 1993 Pastor J. R. Spangler and his wife, Marie, worked with the It Is Written evangelistic series conducted by Mark Finley in the Moscow Olympic Stadium. He and his wife planned to visit the Ukraine again. A number of years after Marie's father died, her mother married Alexander Kubrock, from Yale, Virginia. As a young lad at the turn of the century Kubrock had emigrated to America from the Ukraine and become a Seventh-day Adventist. Because of the Spanglers' close relationship with Marie's stepfather, both of them dreamed of holding meetings in Moscow. During the series Bob Spangler met Sasha.

After the series concluded, the Spanglers were exhausted, and Bob, in particular, wanted to return home. However, Marie insisted that they carry out their original plan of visiting the Ukraine and finding the little town where her stepfather had been born.

They spent two weeks in Kiev, and church officials assigned Sasha as their interpreter. Bob had almost forgotten their previous meeting, but as they traveled together during those two weeks the memory came back. Spangler discovered Sasha's knowledge of Hebrew. It excited him to know that here was a full-blooded Jew who knew the language.

Since Bob headed up Project 66, a Bible translation group sponsored by It Is Written, he decided that Sasha could help translate the Old Testament into modern Russian. During the Communist regime studies of biblical Hebrew, Aramaic, and Greek had been virtually nonexistent.

Spangler immediately contacted M. P. Kulakov, Sr., who was the secretary of the Bible Translation Institute, and informed him of Sasha's abilities. Kulakov, former president of the Euro-Asia Division, had dreamed for years of giving the Russian people an easy-to-read, reliable Russian Bible. The current Synodal version had numerous mistakes. Furthermore, it was 150 years old, and much of the language was difficult for the average person to read. Spangler had joined Kulakov in the project of preparing a new version of the Bible in Russian.

Alexander Bolotnikov now joined the project. He was sponsored to study biblical languages at Andrews University, where he earned a master's degree and became part of the Bible Translation Institute's staff.